Praise for *Injustice in Indian Country*

"In *Injustice in Indian Country,* Amy L. Casselman reveals that the long, ugly and ignoble history of violence against indigenous people is not over, but continues today in the form of rampant sexual violence by non-Native men against Native women. These rarely prosecuted assaults are not the product of aberrant acts by isolated individuals, but rather reflect the cumulative consequences of centuries of legal, social, and administrative policies and practices designed to protect white men from accountability for victimizing Native women. Drawing deftly on ideas and analyses developed by a wide range of indigenous feminist activists and scholars and their allies, Casselman makes an astute and sophisticated case for a comprehensive decolonial and intersectional politics grounded in the direct experiences and articulated aspirations of Native women."

—George Lipsitz, Author of *How Racism Takes Place*

"One of the most significant roles of sovereign nations is to protect the safety of its citizens. This important new work looks deeply into the dynamics of legal and sexual violence created by federal Indian policy. It reframes our understanding of the gendered nature of colonial violence in a poignant and compelling narrative. The author's engaging outline of decolonial frameworks developed by American Indian women makes an essential contribution to anti-violence movements."

—Donna Martinez, Professor and Chair, Ethnic Studies, University of Colorado Denver

"Amy L. Casselman's *Injustice in Indian Country* is a stunning account of one of the most serious yet under-theorized public health crises in the United States. Identifying American colonialism as the most significant pathogen in Indian country, Casselman's moving narrative shows how the egregious practices of the United States don't just contribute to, but in fact cause violence against American Indian women. In demonstrating how criminal jurisdiction impacts mental, physical, and community health, the author brilliantly weaves together personal accounts, political analysis, and modern-day activism, giving us all hope that despite this crisis, justice is possible."

—Alann Salvador, Program Director, Kedren Health

Injustice in Indian Country

CRITICAL INDIGENOUS AND AMERICAN INDIAN STUDIES

Andrew Jolivette
General Editor

Vol. 1

This book is a volume in a Peter Lang monograph series.
Every volume is peer reviewed and meets
the highest quality standards for content and production.

PETER LANG
New York • Bern • Frankfurt • Berlin
Brussels • Vienna • Oxford • Warsaw

Amy L. Casselman

Injustice in Indian Country

Jurisdiction, American Law, and Sexual Violence Against Native Women

PETER LANG
New York • Bern • Frankfurt • Berlin
Brussels • Vienna • Oxford • Warsaw

Library of Congress Cataloging-in-Publication Data

Casselman, Amy L.
Injustice in Indian country: jurisdiction, American law, and sexual violence against native women / Amy L. Casselman.
pages cm. — (Critical indigenous and American Indian studies; vol. 1)
Includes bibliographical references.
1. Criminal jurisdiction—United States. 2. Indians of North America—Legal status, laws, etc. 3. Indians of North America—Criminal justice system.
4. Sex crimes—Law and legislation—United States.
5. Indian women—Crimes against—United States. I. Title.
KIE3336.C37 345.73'0122—dc23 2015016347
ISBN 978-1-4331-3109-7 (hardcover)
ISBN 978-1-4539-1601-8 (e-book)
ISSN 2376-547X (print)
ISSN 2376-5488 (online)

Bibliographic information published by **Die Deutsche Nationalbibliothek**.
Die Deutsche Nationalbibliothek lists this publication in the "Deutsche Nationalbibliografie"; detailed bibliographic data are available on the Internet at http://dnb.d-nb.de/.

The paper in this book meets the guidelines for permanence and durability of the Committee on Production Guidelines for Book Longevity of the Council of Library Resources.

29 Broadway, 18th floor, New York, NY 10006
www.peterlang.com

Printed in Germany

To all missing and murdered women
To survivors
And to all those who fight for justice

Table of Contents

Preface

This book is the culmination of my research as an adjunct professor of Ethnic Studies, as well as my work as a Case Worker for the Washoe Tribe of Nevada and California. As a Case Worker for the Washoe Tribe's Native Temporary Assistance to Needy Families (TANF) Program, I worked both in urban and rural settings to provide comprehensive support services for Native families—the majority of whom were women with young children. My work often put me in a position in which I became a mediator between the very real needs of Native women and the very bureaucratic needs of a federally funded tribal program. Operating from this point of confluence, I found myself constantly negotiating the various ways that individuals and institutions inscribed violence on the Native women I worked with. The federal government, as part of its trust relationship with Native nations, is responsible for providing basic services to Indian people. Yet, I would spend hours trying to find health care for my clients who were uninsured, days attempting to get students with special needs the educational support that they needed, nights trying to find shelter for clients fleeing abusers, and weeks fighting with child protective services who had illegally removed Indian children from their homes.

Throughout these challenges, the strength of my clients was always very clear to me as they survived adversity and exerted agency in their lives. As they navigated complex American institutions to forge a better life for themselves and their children, they continued the spirit of resistance and survival that characterizes generations of women before them. Native women are here today because they and their ancestors survived hundreds of years of federal policies of physical and cultural genocide to the point that their very existence today is a revolutionary act. This spirit of revolution is still here in the myriad ways that Native women survive continued colonization, subvert attempts at genocide, and exert agency in the face of oppression.

It is in this context that I began to learn about jurisdiction in Indian country. In June 2009 I attended the *Women Are Sacred* conference sponsored by Sacred Circle, a South Dakota organization whose goal is to end violence against Native women. There I met with Native activists, organizers, and survivors who were addressing the ways that complicated systems of jurisdictional authority on Native land systematically denied justice to Native women who experienced sexual violence. In integrating this activism with my personal experience as a Case Worker, I began to understand the way that American criminal jurisdiction and sexual violence act not just as legacies of settlement, but as continued projects of colonization. These initial experiences, coupled with my activism in the Native community, form the foundation of this research.

I have a high amount of accountability to, and encouragement from, Native communities in my pursuit of this research topic. Yet, I have the privilege of being able to learn of these things from a distance. While the content of this research is horrifying, I had the privilege of being shocked by it because it is not an experience common to my community. Many Native people I know, while saddened, are not shocked by this information precisely because they have lived it or know someone who has. As you will read, many Native women—especially those in rural areas—simply do not know anyone in their communities who hasn't experienced sexual violence.

Explicit accounts of violence against Native women are not hard to find. And, as a writer, it is tempting to illustrate my points with the most shocking of stories. I also understand, however, that this type of sensationalism can also be a form of revictimization. While scholarship on violence against women, both Native and non-Native, has become effective partly in its ability to illustrate the depravity of these acts, I use personal stories and examples with caution. The experience of sexual violence is intensely personal, yet the adjudication and activism around it is necessarily public. As such, I tread lightly and with much respect regarding the personal stories I share here. For example, the sexual assault of Lavetta Elk (Oglala Lakota) is woven throughout several chapters. While all of the information included about her assault is publically available, I sought out and received permission from Ms. Elk to share it. While it would have been easy to tell her story solely from primary documents, I incorporated her feedback to craft an image of her that was reflective of her own views, experiences, and desires to move forward after her assault. Though difficult, for many Native women sharing their stories is part of a journey in which healing comes not just through the criminal justice system, but also through using their experiences to shape a world in which colonial violence no longer exists. It is with great respect and humility that I offer these stories in the hope that awareness of this issue can aid that journey.

This book pushes the boundaries of simply documenting the epidemic rate of sexual assault against Native women to root this phenomenon in its colonial context. In doing so, I incorporate the perspectives of Native women to propose new solutions that challenge American hegemony. By shifting the focus towards sovereignty, decolonization and accountability, I hope to offer new possibilities in conceptualizing solutions and creating social change.

In addition to being a resource to the Native community, one of the objectives of this research is that non-Native people who read this will not just be shocked by what they discover, but will use this knowledge to understand that this information is relevant to their lives too. While Indian country may seem like another world for some, the United States of America would not be here without it. It was through relocation, genocide, and sexual violence that reservations were created in order to allow non-Native people to live in the Native lands on which they make their homes today. As Sarah Deer (Muscogee Creek) notes, "We also need to acknowledge that the United States was founded, in part, through the use of sexual violence as a tool, that were it not for the widespread rape of Native American women, many of our towns, counties, and states might not exist."[1] And, it is the continued colonization of Native peoples—and the jurisdictional conflicts that are a part of that project—that allows non-Native people to make their lives in a colonized world.

It is my hope that these harsh realities do not depress anyone, but instead encourage everyone to not just act, but to truly *listen*. To my non-Native audience, listen to the stories of Native survivors and be willing to understand their experiences in their own terms. Listen to the way Native nations articulate solutions and support them in the way that they envision healing. Too often attempts at solving problems in Native communities are co-opted by non-Native people who are so invested in what they think is right for others that they prevent true progress from being made. To you I say listen to these stories, and as you move through the world, don't hold on too tightly to what you have received at the expense of what others have lost.

Note

1. Sarah Deer, "Sovereignty of the Soul: Exploring the Intersection of Rape Law Reform and Federal Indian Law," *Suffolk University Law Review* 38 (2005): 459.

Acknowledgments

I extend my deepest thanks to Lavetta Elk for her willingness to share her story of survival and resistance. Thank you Lavetta for giving me this honor. You are an inspiration to me.

I direct particular appreciation to Dr. Andrew Jolivette who supported me throughout the development of this book. Without his support and encouragement, its publication would not have been possible. Thank you to Dr. Falu Bakrania whose guidance in shaping the parameters of this research allowed me to produce theory and knowledge worthy of publication. To my colleagues at the Washoe Tribe of Nevada and California and members of the Bay Area Native community who guided my decision to pursue this topic, I offer this work as part of my commitment to you.

And to my family, friends and partner: thank you for your enduring support and encouragement throughout this intimate process.

CHAPTER ONE

Introduction

> We, collectively, find that we are often in the role of the prey, to a predator society […] This occurs on an individual level, but equally, and more significantly on a societal level.
>
> —Winona LaDuke (Anishinaabe)[1]

Lavetta Elk[2] (Oglala Lakota) grew up on the Pine Ridge Indian Reservation in Wounded Knee, South Dakota.[3] Her life-long ambition was to join the U.S. Army. Hoping to follow in the footsteps of her grandfathers, uncle, and brother who had all served in the military, she stated that she "had a dream of being the first woman in our tiyospaye, in my family, to serve in the army."[4] Lavetta was an excellent student and received a full scholarship at Rockhurst University where she studied medicine in hopes of becoming a nurse in the army. In preparation for a military career, she requested enlistment information and Staff Sergeant Joseph Kopf was assigned to work with her. Although Ms. Elk was planning to finish college before enlisting, information from Sergeant Kopf that there was an opening for a medic position helped sway her decision to drop out of college and return home to Pine Ridge. Ms. Elk returned home and on December 17, 2002, was driven by Sergeant Kopf to Sioux Falls, South Dakota where she underwent a physical examination. After returning home, Sergeant Kopf congratulated Ms. Elk, informing her that she had passed the physical and had been accepted into the military.

On January 7, 2003, Sergeant Kopf arrived at Ms. Elk's home in a government vehicle. He informed her that her paperwork had been lost and that she needed to come with him to resubmit her height and weight. Ms. Elk went with Sergeant Kopf as she had done before. This time, however, Sergeant Kopf did not take her to Sioux Falls. Instead, he drove to a remote part of the reservation, locked Ms. Elk in the car, and sexually assaulted her. There had been no medic position in the army. In reality, Ms. Elk had failed her initial physical examination and had never been accepted into the military.

Ms. Elk survived the attack, but was severely traumatized. In the days following the assault, her family stated that she cried hysterically, took frequent showers, became withdrawn, and severely depressed. She experienced vomiting, insomnia, nightmares, loss of appetite, and body aches. Later, medical experts confirmed that she suffers from Post Traumatic Stress Disorder and depression as the result of the attack.

After Ms. Elk was attacked, she immediately reported the assault to tribal police who took a statement. Because Ms. Elk is Native, but Sergeant Kopf is not, American law prohibited tribal police from prosecuting him. Instead, their only option was to refer the case to federal prosecutors. On April 8, 2003, the United States Department of Justice declined to prosecute Kopf. On April 18, 2003, the U.S. Army found that Sergeant Kopf had "commit[ted] an indecent assault [...] with intent to gratify [his] sexual desires." Despite this, Sergeant Kopf was not prosecuted in military court. He was not even discharged from the U.S. Army. Instead, he was punished with a reduction in rank from Staff Sergeant to Sergeant and was transferred out of the area for three months.

Despite the military's own admission that Sergeant Kopf did, in fact, sexually assault Ms. Elk, both the U.S. government and military refused to prosecute him. Today he is a free man, employed by the federal government. Like the majority of Native women who have been sexually assaulted by non-Native men in Indian country, Lavetta Elk never saw her perpetrator prosecuted. Unlike other women, however, she did get her day in court. While federal declination prevented Kopf from being prosecuted in criminal court, Ms. Elk pursued a civil case. She sued the United States of America for damages from the assault. She is the first Native individual ever to do so.[5] And she won.

On April 28, 2009, in *Lavetta Elk v. the United States,* a federal judge awarded Ms. Elk $590,755.06 in damages. To win her case, Ms. Elk leveraged the 1868 Fort Laramie Treaty[6] that states:

> If bad men among the whites, or among other people subject to the authority of the United States shall commit any wrong upon the person or property of the Indians, the United States will [...] reimburse the injured person for the loss sustained.[7]

Because Ms. Elk is an enrolled member of the Oglala Lakota Nation, she is a beneficiary of the Fort Laramie Treaty. In *Elk v. U.S.*, Judge Francis Allegra noted that the climate of the era in which the Fort Laramie Treaty was signed was one marked by extreme cases of sexual violence against Native women. Citing the Doolittle Report of 1867, which documented the epidemic of sexual assault and mutilation of Native women and children by white Army officers, Allegra noted that the Native signatories of the Fort Laramie Treaty most likely intended passages like the one above to be used to specifically protect Native women from the sexual assault of "bad men among the whites" who clearly posed an incredible danger to Native women at the time. Significantly, just as the treaty was crafted to protect Native women in the 1800s from the predatory violence of white men, it continues to be leveraged to protect Native women from the predatory violence of "bad men among the whites" today.

Like countless other women, the challenge of prosecuting non-Native on Native crime in Indian country contributed to the declination of Ms. Elk's case by federal prosecutors. As Kopf turned his car away from Sioux Falls and instead towards tribal land, he dramatically increased his chances of sexually assaulting Ms. Elk with impunity. And this turned out to be the case. Because Kopf isn't Native, he was immune from tribal jurisdiction. And because both the federal government and the army declined to prosecute him, he will most likely never face criminal charges for his actions. The message sent from both the federal government and the U.S. military's refusal to prosecute Kopf is that what happened to Ms. Elk simply doesn't matter. Though clearly acknowledging that Kopf sexually violated Ms. Elk, the army appeared to value his service more than the experience of Ms. Elk or the lives of all of the women that he will be sure to encounter as a representative of the U.S. Army.

Ms. Elk's experience exemplifies the complex and multilayered phenomenon of sexual assault against Native women in Indian country. On the surface, her story highlights the predatory nature of non-Native assailants who exploit jurisdiction to prey on Native women. Sergeant Kopf is a non-Native man who singled out a Native woman living in Indian country. Ms. Elk entered Sergeant Kopf's vehicle as the result of a plan carefully fabricated by him in order to lure her into his custody. Once Ms. Elk was in his car, he chose to assault her in a remote area of the reservation. Rather than driving to Sioux Falls as they had before, Kopf avoided state land and instead chose to assault Ms. Elk on the reservation, thereby leveraging his privileged racial status to escape prosecution.

But beyond the assault of one man against one woman, the story of Ms. Elk tells a much deeper and nuanced story. Not only was this a predatory sexual attack by a non-Native perpetrator against a Native woman carried out on Native land, but it was also done by a representative of the federal government using government property. Using his power as an officer in the U.S. Army, as well as equipment furnished by the federal government (in this case a military vehicle), Sergeant Kopf's sexual assault of Ms. Elk brings the history of American colonial expansion into the present moment.

In the case of Lavetta Elk, the entire narrative of Euro-American colonization was both literally and figuratively inscribed on her body. The creation of the United States as we know it was made possible through the violent relocation of Native people—including Lavetta's ancestors—to reservations.[8] This violent process was legitimated both through a legal system that viewed Native people as problematic and in need of removal, and through social discourse that constructed Native women as inherently rapable and violable.[9] Rape was a central tool in the relocation of Native people and the creation of reservation land. Yet—in brutal irony—it is specifically *because* Ms. Elk is a Native woman living on Native land, that her assault went unpunished. As such, her case demonstrates the ways that the violence of colonization continues to manifest in Native communities and inscribe violence onto the bodies of Native women.

While Lavetta Elk's assault reveals a deeper history of American colonialism, so too does her activism and personal agency. Just like her ancestors who fought and died to codify their sovereignty, Ms. Elk carried a long tradition of Native resistance into the present by leveraging treaty rights to exert agency in the face of adversity. And in that way, despite the message that was sent by the declination of her case, the message sent by the ruling in *Elk v. U.S.* might speak even louder. From Ms. Elk's victory we can see that Native women and Native communities can subvert colonial power structures to shape their own lives. And though treaties have often been used as a method to oppress Native people (as colonial tools that legitimated U.S. conquest and Indian relocation, and later as documents that were abrogated under continued colonization) *Elk v. U.S.* demonstrates that despite their tenuous history, Native treaties are still legally binding and can be used strategically by the Native community. Operating from this standpoint, and setting a precedent that Native individuals can sue for damages, Ms. Elk has cleared a path for lawsuits that use treaties to address the myriad ways that Native individuals and communities endure lasting pain from historic and contemporary colonization.[10, 11]

The bravery of Ms. Elk to come forward, endure a public trial, and fight for reparations for this traumatic experience has been widely celebrated. Native and non-Native communities alike have applauded this victory as being one for sexual assault survivors, Native women, and Native communities as a whole.[12] According to many in the Native community, this case not only gave Ms. Elk a sense that justice has been served, but also sent an important message to the American public that treaties are still the law of the land and that Native people have the right to sue for pain and suffering under them.[13]

Despite being hailed as a great victory for Native women and the Native community, we must also problematize notions of "justice" and "victory" in *Elk v. U.S.* While Ms. Elk was able to leverage the Fort Laramie Treaty to receive compensation for pain and suffering, Kopf himself was never prosecuted. The federal government and the U.S. Army's failure to pursue the case still sends a powerful message about violence against Native women, and illustrates the impunity with which non-Native men may assault them. After all, Kopf did not pay for his crime—the United States of America did. What many call "justice" for Ms. Elk was in reality *reparations* for an assault that had already been committed. Perhaps true justice for Ms. Elk and others would go beyond reparations or even prosecution. Perhaps true justice would be shaping a world in which sexual violence is not an epidemic within Native communities at all.

Injustice in Indian Country

Violence against Native women is not traditional. Before Europeans arrived in what is now known as the United States of America, sexual violence against Native women was virtually unheard of.[14] In the rare instances in which it did occur, Native communities used their own functioning justice systems to swiftly address the perpetrator and restore balance to the community.[15]

Today, rates of sexual violence against Native women exceed any other demographic in the United States. According to the U.S. Department of Justice, Native women are 2.5 times more likely to be raped than any other woman in America, and 34.1% of Native women will be raped in their lifetimes.[16] While there are no statistics that describe the rates of violence in Indian country specifically, some sources indicate that rates of sexual violence on many reservations are, in fact, much higher than statistics for Native women in general. In some communities, rape has become the number one reported crime.[17] In other Native nations, informal polls in rural areas indicate that up to 100% of Native women interviewed have experienced sexual assault at least once in their lifetime.[18] Referring to the statistic that one in three Native women will be raped in their lifetime, Native journalist Mary Annette Pember notes, "I and all the Indian women I know want to know, however, who those other two women are who haven't been assaulted—because we've never met them. The truth is that it's been open season on Indian women for a very, very long time."[19]

Understanding how sexual assault has transitioned from being virtually non-existent to reaching epidemic levels in Indian country in which it is "open season" on Native women, requires us to confront the project of Euro-American colonization. While westward expansion forced Native people onto the reservations, rancherias, and pueblos that compose modern Indian country,[20] the U.S. federal government also created a series of complex, contradictory, and competing laws that govern who has the authority to manage the people and activity within these spaces. Because of this, when a Native woman is sexually assaulted in or around Indian country, her experiences of the attack and visions for justice are rarely centered by the response of the modern American criminal justice system. Because of the complexity of modern criminal jurisdiction in Indian country, police often marginalize the lived experiences of survivors to instead focus on the jurisdictional determinants of their investigations.

In Indian country, investigating authorities must not only determine the exact location of an assault, but they must also determine the racial identity of both the perpetrator(s) and the victim(s) as well as their relationship to each other and to the community as a whole in order to conclude who has the power to prosecute. Given complicated systems of land ownership in Indian country, as well as unclear definitions of racial identity and relationship status, the challenge of determining these factors often leaves authorities unsure of who has jurisdiction over any given case.[21]

As a result of this complicated system of jurisdiction, sexual predators have learned that Indian country is the most opportune place to prey on women.[22] Non-Native sexual predators like Sergeant Kopf realize that their chances of assaulting someone with impunity dramatically increase when they specifically target a Native woman in Indian country. Here, not only does a complicated system of jurisdictional authority create confusion, but the nature of current jurisdictional law also privileges non-Native identity while simultaneously oppressing Native identity. In Indian country, tribal police are often the only law enforcement agencies for hundreds of miles, yet jurisdictional law makes tribal governments powerless to prosecute most non-Native perpetrators. And, while jurisdiction is relatively straightforward for *non*-Native women who are assaulted in Indian country (with jurisdiction defaulting to the state), the sexual assault of a *Native* woman signals the involvement of three (or more) separate sovereigns. When a Native woman is assaulted, jurisdiction may go to the federal government, the state government, the tribal government, or a combination of the three (and—as in *Elk v. U.S.*—in some cases the military may also step in as a fourth sovereign entity). Determining which combination can be extremely complicated. Often, multiple sovereigns compete for jurisdiction, compromising the investigation of each as evidence is mishandled and perpetrators flee. Alternatively, no sovereign chooses to become involved in the investigation because of real or perceived jurisdictional barriers.[23] Therefore, jurisdictional conflicts do not simply create a climate of impunity in Indian country for men who prey on women in general. Instead, American jurisdiction creates a space in which *non*-Native men often specifically target *Native* women for sexual violence.

As a result, not only do Native women in Indian country have the highest rates of victimization in the nation, they are also the least likely demographic to have their cases of sexual assault investigated, see their perpetrators arrested, and have their cases go to trial. Additionally, while the vast majority of women who experience sexual violence report their attackers as being of the same race, Native women are the one glaring exception.[24] Instead, 86% of Native women who are raped describe their attacker as a non-Native man, and 80% of Native women who survive sexual assault report that their attacker is white.[25, 26]

Native scholar and activist Winona LaDuke tells us that Native women are often in the role of prey to predators.[27] This is clearly illustrated by the climate of impunity in Indian country in which Native women are specifically targeted. However, LaDuke also reminds us that this predation occurs on "an individual level, but equally, and more significantly on a societal level." When a non-Native man specifically targets a Native woman in Indian country for sexual assault because jurisdictional conflicts allow him to, we must contextualize these conflicts in a larger narrative of predatory violence that occurs on a societal level. Rather than occurring as an *individual* pathology in which sexual predators manipulate jurisdiction to get away with sexual assault, jurisdiction in the prosecution of sexual violence against Native women must be read as part of a *colonial* pathology that has *always* constructed Native women as inherently rapable and violable.

As this book will show, Euro-American colonization has always been characterized by both legal and sexual violence. Since first contact, law has been used as a means to legitimate the theft of Native resources and control Native communities.[28] Similarly, the construction of Native women as inherently rapable by white men has also been used as a weapon in the colonial project that seeks to disappear Native peoples as a whole.[29] So important were both legal and sexual violence to the project of American colonization that they, in fact, became enmeshed. Throughout the history of Euro-American colonization, sexual violence became central to federal law and policy, while federal law and policy itself became structured by the logic of sexual violence.

Significantly—and not coincidentally—it is at the crossroads of both legal and sexual violence that we find jurisdictional conflicts in Indian country today. Legal violence that legitimated the dispossession and relocation of Native peoples, coupled with sexual violence against Native women as a tool of colonization, has created Indian country as we know it.[30] And today, it is in these colonial spaces that federal Indian policy has made it exceedingly difficult to prosecute sexual violence against Native women. Today in Indian country, sexual assault becomes a twice-told tale of colonial violence: the history of colonization which became possible because of the rape of Native women by white men, continues—through jurisdictional conflicts—to construct colonial spaces in which Native women are again sexually assaulted by non-Native men with impunity. In this way, we must read modern jurisdictional conflicts as both *shaped by* a history of sexual and legal violence while also *shaping* the experience of violence in Native communities. Therefore, I argue modern jurisdictional conflicts in Indian country are not only *legacies* of colonialism, but actively *maintain* and *inscribe* colonial violence on the bodies of Native women.

Despite the clear relationship between colonization, sexual violence, and the law, a comprehensive body of work has yet to contextualize American jurisdiction within a colonial narrative while incorporating Native women as active agents. This book challenges dominant approaches that marginalize Native communities and fail to historicize jurisdictional conflicts by tracing a historical legacy of colonization while centering the experiences of Native women and communities. In doing so, this book generates awareness of American jurisdiction in the prosecution of sexual violence in Indian country, addresses the shortcomings of existing scholarship, and contributes to an emerging body of literature that theorizes race, gender, violence, and colonization using an intersectional approach.

Chapter Two reviews the scholarly literature that discusses federal Indian policy, violence against Native women, and methods to address jurisdiction in Indian country. Here, I explore the ways that scholarship has consistently divorced jurisdictional conflicts from their colonial context while marginalizing the experience of Native women and communities. I also discuss the methodological interventions I have crafted in order to address these shortcomings.

Chapter Three explores the major pieces of federal law and policy that have created the modern jurisdictional schema in Indian country. By historicizing jurisdictional conflicts in the context of these pieces, I argue that rather than emerging from the benign neglect of the federal government, jurisdictional conflicts have emerged from a colonial narrative that consistently invests in white American hegemony while divesting in Native sovereignty. In demonstrating the common colonial themes that emerge from their creation, I argue that jurisdictional conflicts must themselves be read in this colonial context—and that when jurisdictional conflicts operate in Indian country, that they themselves are characterized by these colonial themes.

Chapter Four illustrates the way that jurisdictional conflicts in Indian country affect Native women today. Taking my point of departure from literature that is often uncritical of the colonial context of violence, Chapter Four also explores the history of sexual assault against Native women under colonization, highlighting the ways that sexual and legal violence became enmeshed historically. In doing so, Chapter Four demonstrates that jurisdictional conflicts are part of a larger colonial narrative that has always viewed Native women as inherently violable. From this, I support my thesis that jurisdictional conflicts are not simply part of a colonial legacy—rather, they maintain and inscribe colonial violence on the bodies of Native women in Indian country.

Chapters Five and Six shift the focus from identifying problems to forging solutions. These chapters examine the Tribal Law and Order Act of 2010 (TLOA) and the Violence Against Women Reauthorization Act of 2013 (VAWA 2013) to identify the ways that the federal government has framed solutions to jurisdictional conflicts. As the most recent manifestations of federal Indian policy that also purport to solve jurisdictional problems and sexual violence against Native women, attention to the TLOA and VAWA 2013 is important in that it has the power to reveal how the federal government may or may not continue to invest in white American hegemony while marginalizing Native communities. In measuring the TLOA and VAWA 2013 against the federal Indian policies discussed in Chapter Three, Chapters Five and Six begin to contemplate the possibility of legislating solutions to the problem of jurisdiction and sexual violence in a way that both invests in and enfranchises Native communities.

As a concluding chapter, Chapter Seven surveys approaches to solving jurisdictional conflicts and sexual violence against Native women to understand how various forms of resistance create possibilities for social change. Focusing on the lived experiences of Native women and solutions that center Native communities, this chapter highlights the tension within the Native anti-violence movement over the role that colonial power structures should play in crafting solutions. While some scholars argue that American institutions can never be effective in solving jurisdictional problems, this chapter uses Chela Sandoval's theory of differential consciousness and Kevin Bruyneel's theory of a "third space" of sovereignty to give credence to strategies that Native women like Lavetta Elk use to strategically leverage colonial power structures to shape their own lives. Using Native activist Sarah Deer's essay "What She Say, It Be Law," I argue that the best solutions to jurisdictional conflicts and sexual violence against Native women come from honoring the diverse experiences and visions for justice of Native women themselves.

A Note on Specificity

This project recognizes the heterogeneity of the Indigenous population of the United States and makes every effort to discuss Native nations in terms of their individual and unique histories under colonization. However, despite the incredible diversity of Native nations, federal Indian policy has insisted on collapsing ethnic identity into a monolithic racial category, often referring to all Native people as "Indians." Thus, while this book recognizes the unique character of each Native nation, its discussion of jurisdiction and federal Indian policy has the tendency to homogenize all Native nations precisely because the federal government itself does so. In other words, while I am loathe to speak of Native people and Native nations as having a common colonial identity, the fact that federal Indian policy often makes laws that apply to all "Indians," "tribes," and "Indian country," requires me to speak in generalities when discussing the ways that jurisdiction operates in the lives of Native women.

Additionally, jurisdiction in Indian country affects other crimes besides sexual violence. Any "major crime"[31] in Indian country (including felonies like murder, kidnapping and arson) also signals the involvement of multiple sovereigns that often conflict and subsequently marginalize Native people. I have chosen to focus on sexual violence against Native women for several reasons. As I have mentioned, rape has become the number one crime in many Native communities. Sexual violence against Native women has reached epidemic levels that often exceed those of other crimes in Indian country. As such, it necessitates specific attention. Furthermore, examining sexual violence against Native women in Indian country in the context of modern jurisdictional conflicts facilitates a nuanced discussion of the way that both legal and sexual violence have operated under colonization. Finally, while there is much awareness of the high rates of poverty and violence in American Indian communities, the systematic denial of justice to Native women and the systematic privileging of non-Native identity in crimes of sexual assault is only beginning to garner attention outside of Native communities. As such, this text aims to promote awareness of an important social problem with the possibility of mobilizing a broad base of constituents to address it.

A Note on Terminology

I define "jurisdictional conflicts" as any instance in which overlapping or competing authority by federal, state, and/or tribal entities delays or denies justice to a Native woman who has experienced sexual violence. This includes occasions in which multiple entities compete for jurisdiction, compromising the investigation of each, as well as instances in which no entity exercises jurisdiction. I consciously engage the term "conflict" in this discussion both because jurisdiction in Indian country often signals a conflict between competing sovereigns, but also because jurisdiction in Indian country signals violent conflicts between bodies. Acknowledging the way that jurisdiction plays a significant role in the epidemic levels of interracial violence against Native women in Indian country, the term "jurisdictional conflict" is meant to invoke larger colonial discussions of power, sovereignty, and violence.

This text uses a variety of terms to refer to the Indigenous people of what is now known as the United States of America. Many Native people conceptualize themselves as citizens of their own Native nations, and as such I make an effort to frame identities in terms of individual membership. When referring to individuals broadly, I employ the term "Native" to indicate those who identify as being Indigenous to the United States. This term, however, is fluid throughout the text, always with attention to the way that individuals and communities self-identify. Furthermore, for the purposes of discussing federal legislation, I sometime use the term "Indian" as this is still the legal term the federal government uses to refer to Native people.

Prior to colonization, Indigenous peoples existed as sovereign, autonomous nations with their own laws, policies, governments and territories. As such, I choose to use the term "Native nations" rather than "tribe" when referring to communities of Indigenous peoples. However, at times it is valuable to employ the term "tribe" or "tribal," especially as it relates to definitions under federal law. Furthermore, some Native communities prefer to use the word "tribe" rather than "nation." Such is the case for the community in which I worked, the Washoe Tribe of Nevada and California. At all times in this research, I strive to use terminology that reflects self-identification and the wishes of individuals and communities.

Furthermore, to emphasize the agency of Native women, this research makes a conscious effort to refer to those who experience sexual violence as "survivors." Often, Native women who experience sexual violence are referred to as "victims," and are constructed as passive subjects. While the colonial context of jurisdiction in Indian country often demonstrates the way that Native women are systematically marginalized by federal Indian policy, to portray Native women as passive victims is incorrect. The goal of this research is to show how Native women do not just survive sexual violence, but that they play a meaningful role in navigating colonial power structures to shape their own lives and agitate for social change. Unfortunately however, we also know that not all women who experience sexual assault survive. Statistics show that as part of the climate of impunity in Indian country, sexual assault against Native women is not only more prevalent, but more violent. When compared to non-Native women, Native women in the U.S. are more likely to be sexually assaulted by multiple perpetrators, are more likely to have their sexual assault result in a completed rape, are more likely to have their perpetrator use a weapon, and are more likely to suffer physical injuries and hospitalization in addition to the assault.[32] As a result, some Native women do not survive their sexual assaults. Therefore, at times it becomes necessary for me to refer to Native women as victims. But I use this term with caution, and always with an attempt to emphasize the agency of each woman in every case.

What Is Justice?

This text argues that jurisdictional conflicts in the prosecution of sexual violence systematically deny justice to Native women in Indian country. As such, it is important to discuss what I mean by "justice" in this piece. Western notions of law and order often frame justice in terms of arrest, prosecution and incarceration. Though laws in Indian country often allow non-Native perpetrators to avoid arrest and conviction, it is limiting to frame justice solely in these terms. As Cherokee scholar Andrea Smith points out, the Western criminal justice system only functions at the point of crisis after violence in communities has already happened.[33] Thus, part of conceptualizing justice for Native women must focus on the crisis itself. Facilitating the arrest of non-Native perpetrators might reduce the rates of interracial sexual assault against Native women, but would still leave the colonial context of violence intact. Therefore, this research also incorporates broader conceptualizations of justice that address the context of violence and the need for Native communities to heal from historical trauma.

Cherokee activist Jacqueline Agtuca reminds us that ultimately, justice must be articulated from Native women themselves.[34] Though many scholars claim that Native women should find justice either entirely within the Western criminal justice system, or entirely outside of it,[35] this research reveals that justice to Native women is more complex and can be comprised of many things. Often, to Native women "justice" includes using the Western criminal justice system while also working simultaneously to shape a world in which that justice system is no longer a part of Native communities.[36] As such, I make every effort to honor the diverse voices, experiences, and articulations of individuals and communities themselves when discussing justice. It is with this survivor-centered and community-centered approach that we can begin to frame notions of justice in the face of what is clearly an incredible injustice in Indian country.

Notes

1. As quoted in Devon Abbott Mihesuah, *Indigenous American Women: Decolonization, Empowerment, Activism* (Lincoln: University of Nebraska Press, 2003): 41.
2. Information regarding Ms. Elk is gathered from publically available sources. Additionally, Ms. Elk gave her consent to have her story shared in this book.
3. Unless otherwise noted, all facts pertaining to Lavetta Elk are found in *Lavetta Elk v. the United States*, No. 05–186L. U.S. Court of Federal Claims. 28 Apr. 2009.
4. Jim Kent, "Lakota Woman Accuses U.S. Army Recruiter of Sexual Assault; Forfeits Full College Scholarship to 'Live Her Dream,'" *News From Indian Country* 2 Jun. 2003: 10A.
5. "Miami Attorney Wins Unprecedented Sex Case Using 1868 Indian Treaty." *SNAP*. 2009.
6. 1868 treaty guaranteeing land ownership, hunting rights, and jurisdictional authority among other things (15 Stat. 635. 29 Apr. 1868). See Appendix B: Law and Policy Reference.
7. Quoted in *Elk v. U.S.*
8. Deer, "Sovereignty of the Soul" 458.
9. Ibid. See also Andrea Smith, *Conquest: Sexual Violence and American Indian Genocide* (Cambridge: South End Press, 2005).
10. For example, the Elk decision invites Native nations with similar treaties to sue the federal government for pain and suffering caused by Indian boarding schools.
11. Bill Donovan, "S.D. Court Case May Allow Claims Against the U.S.," *Navajo Times* 7 May 2009: A4.
12. Matthew Gruchow, "Native Woman Wins Unprecedented Case," *Ojibwe News* 1 May 2009: 1–2; SNAP, "Miami Attorney."
13. Ibid.
14. Hilary Weaver, "The Colonial Context of Violence," *Journal of Interpersonal Violence* 24.9 (2009): 1555.
15. Ibid.
16. 2004 United States Department of Justice Statistics as quoted in Amnesty International *Maze of Injustice: The Failure to Protect Indigenous Women from Sexual Violence in the USA* (New York: Amnesty International Publications, 2007) 2. See also Patricia Tjaden and Nancy Thoennes, "Full Report of the Prevalence, Incidence, and Consequences of Violence Against Women," a study prepared at the National Institute of Justice, Office of Justice Programs, U.S. Department of Justice. NCJ 183781. Nov. 2004.
17. Paula Gunn Allen, "Violence and the American Indian Woman," *The Speaking Profits Us: Violence in the Lives of Women of Color*, ed. Maryviolet C. Burns (Seattle: Center for the Prevention of Sexual and Domestic Violence, 1986) 6.
18. Eleanor Ned-Sunnyboy, "Special Issues Facing Alaska Native Women Survivors of Violence," *Sharing Our Stories of Survival*, eds. Sarah Deer, Bonnie Clairmont et al. (New York: Altamira Press, 2007) 72.
19. Mary Annette Pember, "Tribes Gain New Clout Against Crime," *Daily Yonder*. Web. 12 Aug. 2010. <dailyyonder.com/tribes-gain-new-clout-against-crime/2010/08/11/2884> Accessed 12 Apr. 2011.

20. "Indian country" is the legal term used by the federal government to refer to "all land within the limits of any Indian reservation under the jurisdiction of the United States government." This definition also includes land within the bounds of other dependent Indian communities including pueblos and rancherias, as well as Indian allotments and Indian titles to lands outside of reservations. See 18 U.S.C § 1151. For a glossary of terms used in this research see Appendix A: Glossary of Terms.
21. Amnesty International, *Maze.*
22. Louis Gray, "Protecting Indian Women Vital For Native Communities," *Native American Times* 14 Oct, 2005: 8.
23. Amnesty International, *Maze.*
24. 2004 USDOJ statistics as quoted in Amnesty International, *Maze* 4–5.
25. Ibid. See also Steven Perry, "Measuring Crime and Justice in Indian Country," *Bureau of Justice Statistics* 9 Dec. 2004: 9–10.
26. I acknowledge that not all cases of sexual violence consist of a male perpetrator and a female victim. Sexual violence can happen between men, between women, and between a female perpetrator and a male victim. This research focuses on male perpetrated sexual violence against Native women because it characterizes the majority of sexual assaults in Indian country, as well as reflects the history of Euro-American colonization. Further research is needed to examine the way that other types of sexual assault may shape the lives of Native people in Indian country.
27. See epigraph.
28. Ward Churchill, *Perversions of Justice: Indigenous Peoples and Angloamerican Law* (San Francisco: City Lights Books, 2003).
29. Smith, *Conquest*; Brenda Hill, "The Role of Advocates in the Tribal Legal System: Context is Everything," *Sharing Our Stories of Survival.*
30. Deer, "Sovereignty of the Soul."
31. For more on this, see Chapter Three.
32. Tjaden and Thoennes, "Full Report" 51–56.
33. Smith, *Conquest* 169.
34. Jacqueline Agtuca, "Beloved Women: Life Givers, Caretakers, Teachers of Future Generations," *Sharing Our Stories of Survival* 4–5.
35. For more on this, see Chapters Two and Six.
36. Agtuca, "Beloved Women."

CHAPTER TWO

Literature Review and Methodology

To demonstrate the unique contributions of this research, this chapter explores three important bodies of scholarship central to addressing jurisdictional conflicts in the prosecution of sexual violence against Native women in Indian country: federal Indian law and policy; sexual violence against Native women; and agency and self-determination strategies in Native communities. In this chapter, I argue that existing scholarship fails to contextualize jurisdictional conflicts in a history of colonial violence while framing solutions that enfranchise the Native community. As I review each body of work, I use its shortcomings to craft effective methodological interventions that enable me to fully theorize American jurisdiction and sexual violence in Indian country while centering the experiences of Native women.

Framing Jurisdiction Under Federal Indian Policy

The majority of scholarship on federal Indian policy focuses on the first few centuries of federal-Indian relations. Sources that are critical of these eras theorize early federal Indian policy as something that has served to both legitimate U.S. hegemony and justify westward expansion.[1] Because of the focus on these eras, accounts of the way that the federal government has used policy to legitimate the

American settler-state often appear as rooted in the past. In the wake of growing U.S. hegemony, few scholars have carried this narrative of conquest through more recent history and into the present moment.

With the emergence of American Indian Studies as a discipline, we begin to see scholars theorize the way that colonization has informed more recent federal Indian policy.[2] This body of literature demonstrates the way that federal Indian policy from contact to present has consistently been used as a tool to divest Native nations of their land and ability to self-govern. Here we see that federal Indian policy—often under the guise of reciprocity and mutual interest—has consistently been drafted in order to protect the interests and welfare of white Americans while systematically divesting Native peoples of meaningful self-determination.[3] When discussing this process in the context of Indian country jurisdiction, some scholars explain divestments in Native sovereignty and investments in white American hegemony by arguing that the federal government feared what they perceived to be inferior tribal justice systems.[4] This body of theory sees U.S. federal Indian law as always working to protect non-Native (read: white) bodies from the perceived violence of Native bodies as well as the so-called inferiority of Native standards of justice.[5]

Scholars who discuss jurisdictional conflicts often cite divestments in tribal sovereignty as factors in their creation, yet stop short of incorporating a critical analysis of U.S. federal Indian policy itself.[6] Rather than trace the evolution of jurisdictional conflicts to target colonialism and paternalism as areas to address, most literature focuses on ways to solve these issues from a legal perspective. This body of literature is most often found in legal studies journals and is written by non-Native scholars theorizing from a U.S. judicial perspective. In this trope, jurisdictional conflicts are always seen as problematic for the legal system in general, but not specifically for the tribal nations and Native people that fall victim to them.[7] Here, concepts of justice are always articulated with the U.S. nation-state at the center. From this perspective, Native survivors and tribal governments are marginalized or non-existent.

One example that typifies a legal studies approach to jurisdictional conflicts is Kevin Meisner's "Modern Problems of Criminal Jurisdiction in Indian Country."[8] Meisner's work is typical of legal scholarship in his characterization of jurisdictional conflicts as unfortunate—yet inevitable—consequences of a complicated judicial system that he is generally uncritical of. Like a multitude of law review pieces that make similar claims,[9] Meisner's work places the onus of responsibility on the nation-state, yet encourages hegemonic structures of justice that mirror the U.S. legal system. For example, in the section that examines solutions to jurisdictional conflicts, every single suggestion is framed either in terms of additional ways that the U.S. federal government should regulate tribal legal systems, or in terms of ways tribal governments can emulate hegemonic structures of governance to alleviate jurisdictional conflicts.

Moving away from the trope of legal studies that pathologizes non-hegemonic legal structures is the body of literature that attempts to place Native nations in a more central position. Though Amnesty International is not a scholarly entity, their publication *Maze of Injustice: The Failure to Protect Indigenous Women from Sexual Violence in the USA,* actually begins to theorize and center not just tribal governments, but also Native women when analyzing jurisdictional conflicts.[10]

Significant as the first comprehensive mainstream body of literature that focuses on the effects of jurisdictional conflicts on Native women in Indian country, *Maze* documents the ways that jurisdictional conflicts have evolved while placing their findings in the context of U.S. colonialism. Though this approach is impressive, Amnesty International's piece is representative of a problematic liberal approach to jurisdictional conflicts. Throughout the piece, Amnesty International takes a step in the right direction by critiquing colonialism and moving Native women and tribal governments away from the margins. However, *Maze,* as well as other pieces within the liberal feminist canon, does not truly center tribal governments in its critique of jurisdictional conflicts. In *Maze,* suggestions include encouraging the federal government to work with input from tribal governments in drafting solutions to jurisdictional conflicts. Placing the federal government in the center and encouraging them to work *with* the *input* of tribal governments, still places the power to address the problem squarely on the shoulders of the very entity that created the problem in the first place. Though Amnesty International and others' attempts at placing tribal interests within the discussion may represent a step in the right direction, there is no comprehensive theoretical body of literature that truly centers tribal agencies and Native communities in addressing jurisdictional conflicts.

In order to address the gaps that I have identified in existing scholarship, my work analyzes federal law and policy, Supreme Court rulings, treaties, case studies, and legal precedents to locate instances in which the federal government has divested tribal nations of their ability to exercise self-determination over their own lands and peoples. Specifically, I locate areas in which these divestments clearly lead to the creation of jurisdictional conflicts. In doing so, I place the onus of responsibility for the creation of these conflicts squarely on the shoulders of the U.S. federal government. Using the Thomas database,[11] transcripts of senate floor debates, news articles, as well as secondary sources, I analyze the discourse surrounding federal Indian policy to more deeply theorize the laws that have created jurisdictional conflicts.

This work places tribal governments, community organizations and Native women in the center of analysis. I do so by using primary historical documents that include Native voices (such as newspaper articles and other publications), secondary sources that discuss historical sources (including scholarly work that uses historical primary documents), and current publications (including Native websites, current news articles, Native blogs and magazines) to discuss ways in which Native women and communities conceptualize how jurisdictional conflicts have been created and maintained.

For the purposes of this research, I consider voices to be "Native" when the speaker self-identifies as Native (as in online blogs) or are cited as Native (by the author of news articles for example). I consider sources to be "Native" when published or produced by Native nations themselves, by community organizations run by Native nations, or by organizations run by a cohort of Native individuals. Examples include *Indian Country Today Media Network* (a Native run online periodical), *Restoration of Native Sovereignty and Safety for Native Women Magazine* (published by Sacred Circle, an organization founded and operated by Native women), and publications by the Tribal Law and Policy Institute, Cangleska, and Mending the Sacred Hoop Technical Assistance Project (all run and operated by Native individuals and groups).

By centering Native communities while investigating how jurisdictional conflicts are shaped by colonialism, narratives of paternalism, and historical forms of violence, I can thoroughly interrogate jurisdictional conflicts as colonial phenomena and address the shortcomings in existing literature.

Race, Gender and Colonization: Intersectionality in Sexual Violence Against Native Women

At the heart of jurisdictional conflicts in the prosecution of sexual violence against Native women are the intersections of gender, race, and violence. While traditional feminist scholarship has often treated each of these issues separately, more recent literature has attempted to theorize the way that these complex intersections have operated in the lives of women of color.[12] Subverting dominant paradigms of gender oppression that ignore race, and theories of racial oppression that ignore gender, intersectional scholarship demonstrates the ways that race and gender operate *simultaneously* when discussing violence against women of color. For example, in her piece "Mapping the Margins: Intersectionality, Identity Politics, and Violence Against Women of Color," Kimberlé Crenshaw expertly demonstrates how violence affects women of color differently from their white counterparts. For example, while both white women and women of color are affected by domestic violence, women of color are less likely to be able to secure employment, affordable housing, and educational opportunities that allow them to live independently of their abusers. Additionally, racialized oppression makes many women of color less able to use resources like domestic violence shelters and the criminal justice system because of language barriers and immigration status.[13]

While theorizing women of color's experiences as qualitatively different than white women is an important step, it is also limited. Though Native women recognize the need to theorize the intersections of race and gender, many have shown that the experiences of Native women are also qualitatively different from both white women *and* other women of color.[14] Here, Native women assert that theorizing the intersection of race and gender, while important, doesn't always account for colonial oppression and the way that it operates differently in the lives of Native women specifically.[15]

Working within the paradigm of Native feminism are Native scholars who view sexual violence against Native women through a lens that shows how gender, racial and *colonial* oppression are operating simultaneously in the lives of Native women. While previous models may have stressed an additive approach to racial and gendered oppression, or an intersectional approach that ignored colonial violence, new scholarship shows how Native women are operating within colonial relationships to the nation-state that themselves are simultaneously gendered and racialized.[16] This new framework, emerging from the work of women of color scholars and feminist studies, represents a significant paradigm shift in the way that sexual violence against Native women is theorized.

While many Native women write from an intersectional perspective that includes colonial violence,[17] the publication of Andrea Smith's *Conquest: Sexual Violence and American Indian Genocide* was the first time that intersections of sex, gender, colonial violence and Native identity were theorized in a comprehensive body of academic literature. *Conquest* represents a watershed moment in the way that American Indian Studies theorizes the experiences of Native women. Building off of other theorists who have demonstrated the way that Native women's bodies have been constructed as dirty and valueless,[18] Smith shows how under colonization, the U.S. nation-state has consistently viewed Native bodies as inherently rapable and violable. Using colonial patriarchal gender violence as a theoretical framework, Smith goes on to show the myriad ways that violence manifests in the lives of Native women.

Though Smith makes incredible headway in expanding our understanding of the role of violence in American colonization, her discussion of interpersonal violence at times falls into the same homogenizing trap of other theorists. Like Crenshaw who theorized violence against women of color as almost exclusively domestic intra-racial violence, Smith also tends to characterize interpersonal violence against Native women as almost exclusively between domestic partners. While Smith's work represents a radical shift in the way that we theorize violence, she and other women who have built on her intersectional framework, have reproduced scholarship that considers sexual violence against Native women in terms of monolithic categories of "Native women," "interpersonal violence," and "perpetrators."[19] Here, interpersonal "violence against Native women," often becomes exclusively about *domestic* violence against a homogenous "Native woman" perpetrated by *Native* men.

While intra-racial domestic violence in Native communities is an important issue, the temptation to discuss *all* interpersonal violence in the lives of Native women as perpetrated by Native domestic partners has caused the literature to undertheorize the experiences of sexual violence against Native women. Rarely does anyone look at the multiplicities of experiences within each of these categories or the way that these multiplicities come together to create entirely new scenarios outside of the domestic violence paradigm. Despite the overwhelming statistics that indicate the majority of sexual predators against Native women are *non*-Native men, most literature insists on focusing on domestic violence perpetrated by *Native* men. Rarely do scholars look at the *predatory* violence of *non*-Native perpetrators who prey on Native women, or the way that this violence manifests in Indian country as opposed to urban areas.

To address the aforementioned shortcomings, I use statistics published by the U.S. Department of Justice, the National Crime Victimization Survey, as well as both formally and informally collected statistics gathered in Indian country to feature the diversity within the categories of "violence," "Native women," and "perpetrators." Using these statistics I also demonstrate that non-domestic sexual violence against Native women in Indian country by non-Native perpetrators is a significant source of violence against Native women. Building on the intersectionality framework that Andrea Smith and others use, I theorize interracial sexual violence in Indian country from an intersectional approach. Utilizing this framework, I ground my analysis in a discussion of federal Indian policy, highlighting a master narrative of sexual and legal violence under colonization. In doing so, I build on existing scholarship to highlight the heterogeneity of sexual violence against Native women vis-à-vis American jurisdiction.

American Jurisdiction and Federal Indian Policy: Exerting Agency and Creating Social Change

When addressing jurisdictional conflicts and discussing solutions to sexual violence in Indian country, subject positionality emerges as an important factor. As I have shown, the majority of non-Native legal scholarship discusses the problem uncritically, divorcing it from a colonial context.[20] In refusing to situate jurisdictional conflicts within a colonial narrative, solutions in this trope are often framed ahistorically in ways that center the federal government while marginalizing Native nations.

Because these sources refuse to address the problematic laws and policies that have created jurisdictional conflicts in the first place, non-Native legal scholarship often suggests additional federal policy be enacted to address issues with Indian country jurisdiction.[21] From this perspective, rather than dismantle the problematic legislation that has directly created jurisdictional conflicts, or center Native sovereignty in conceptualizing solutions, non-Native legal scholarship instead frames solutions in terms of enacting additional laws that govern jurisdiction and encouraging Native nations to model themselves after Western legal systems.[22]

In this body of literature, scholars argue for additional laws that regulate communication between federal, state and tribal entities,[23] increased federal presence in Indian country,[24] increased funding for the prison industrial complex,[25] enhancements to existing laws and policies,[26] federal training for tribal police officers,[27] and laws that force state governments to intervene in Indian country.[28] By ignoring the colonial context in which sexual violence and jurisdictional conflicts have emerged, these arguments all frame solutions with the federal government in the center. Rather than look to the communities for whom these solutions matter the most, this trope instead focuses on the federal government as the arbiter of justice in Indian country.

While dominant legal scholarship often ignores the agency of Native nations when discussing solutions to jurisdictional conflicts, some non-Native legal scholarship has begun to incorporate Native nations as potential agents.[29] Departing from scholarship that centers the federal government only, these approaches examine what Native nations themselves can do to address jurisdictional conflicts. Unfortunately, these solutions are limited and hegemonizing insofar as they recommend that Native nations imitate American justice systems in an attempt to gain more power to adjudicate crime. These approaches suggest that since Native nations are denied sovereignty because of a fear that their justice systems are inferior, "elevating" themselves to the level of Western jurisprudence will help them regain the ability to manage crime in their own communities. Here, the only kind of Native sovereignty that is seen as effective in addressing jurisdiction and sexual violence is one that has been co-opted and colonized by Western justice systems themselves.

Given the incredibly problematic way that many non-Native legal scholars have framed approaches to jurisdictional conflicts, most Native scholars argue for radically different solutions. Here, they tend to focus on Native-centered notions of sovereignty in their approach to addressing the issue. Cherokee scholar Andrea Smith is a central figure in the body of literature that argues for a Native-centered anti-violence movement. Taking her point of departure from the problematic legal scholarship described above, she argues for solutions that work entirely outside of the federal government that subvert and dismantle colonial power structures themselves.

Urging us to reconsider using the federal government to address a problem created by the federal government, Smith, together with INCITE!—an organization of women of color against violence co-founded by Smith—advocate for organizing entirely outside of colonial institutions to address sexual violence against Native women.[30] Demonstrating that American colonization is the root cause of the oppression of Native women, both Smith and INCITE! vehemently oppose solutions to violence against Native women that include working within state or federal power structures. As such, both deny the legitimacy of the Western legal system, legislative approaches to solving jurisdictional conflicts, and the prison industrial complex as a means to regulate law and order in Indian country. Additionally, in INCITE!'s *The Revolution Will Not Be Funded: Beyond the Non-Profit Industrial Complex,* Smith and other contributors deny the legitimacy of what they term the "non-profit industrial complex." Here, Smith and INCITE! describe non-profit organizations as extensions of U.S. hegemony. Commenting on the contradiction of using federal funding to liberate oneself from the oppression of the nation-state, the authors make a convincing case that Native women cannot begin to decolonize when using funding from the so-called non-profit industrial complex.

While Smith and INCITE! give a much needed critique to legal scholarship, their approach at times marginalizes their own constituents. Smith's analysis, which is hostile towards those who at times work within existing power structures fails to give credence to many of the Native women and Native community organizations who work to confront the injustices that result from American law and policy. Though many Native women and Native nations do not see solutions to violence as coming from within colonial institutions, to demand that Native women and communities work entirely outside of these structures precludes a vision of justice for Native women who see strategically leveraging these systems as part of a decolonial strategy that shapes a future in which these structures might not exist.

Smith and INCITE!'s approach marginalizes Native women who articulate justice knowing that their perpetrators are incarcerated and can never hurt them again, Native women who do transformational anti-violence work with the aid of federal grants, and Native activists who lobby Congress for legislation that invests in tribal sovereignty while simultaneously embracing decolonial strategies that reject the legitimacy of the federal government as a whole. Though Smith and INCITE!'s work is important in the way that it centers Native women's agency while being critical of the nation-state, it excludes an approach that may on one hand strategically use resources within existing power structures, while also simultaneously working towards a liberation that ultimately does not include them. In Smith and INCITE!'s work we see a disconnect between ideology and praxis, and more work needs to be done to examine the way that Native women and Native community organizations work both within and outside of existing power structures to exert agency in their lives.

This research emerges from the tension between scholars that envision hegemonic solutions to jurisdictional conflicts and activists that frame solutions to sexual violence as entirely outside of American institutions. While non-Native legal scholars consistently advocate working solely within federal hegemony, and some Native scholarship demands that activists work completely outside of colonial institutions, few scholars give credence to those who work both outside and within power structures to shape a future that is free from jurisdictional colonialism and sexual violence.

In contrast, this book draws upon examples of Native community organizations and Native women who have confronted jurisdictional conflicts from a multifaceted approach. Using Chela Sandoval's theory of differential consciousness and Kevin Bruyneel's concept of the "third space" of sovereignty, I analyze these examples to show that Native women and Native community organizations strategically navigate colonial institutions to create social change and shape their own lives. Centering the potential of strategic navigation amid and amongst competing power structures, I examine areas in which Native women and community organizations leverage a variety of resources to confront jurisdictional conflicts and address violence in their communities. Specifically, I examine the Tribal Law and Order Act of 2010 and the Violence Against Women Reauthorization Act of 2013 to explore how the federal government frames jurisdictional conflicts and sexual violence today, how these responses fit within a master narrative of federal Indian policy, and how Native women and Native communities conceptualize, problematize, and strategically navigate these Acts. I also examine *Lavetta Elk v.*

the United States to explore how Native women maneuver among competing power structures to create a platform for broader social change. Finally, I incorporate a discussion of Sarah Deer's essay "What She Say, It Be Law," to discuss the importance of honoring the voices of all Native women and their diverse understandings of justice and healing in the context of jurisdictional conflicts and sexual violence.

Notes

1. See for example: David E. Stannard, *American Holocaust: The Conquest of the New World* (New York: Oxford University Press, 1992); Dee Brown, *Bury My Heart at Wounded Knee: An Indian History of the American West* (New York: Holt, Rinehart & Winston, 1970).
2. See for example: Churchill, *Perversions of Justice*; Vine Deloria and Clifford Lytle, *American Indians, American Justice* (Austin: University of Texas Press, 1983).
3. Ibid.
4. Sidner Larson, "Making Sense of Federal Indian Law," *Wicazo Sa Review* 19.1 (2005) 12.
5. See for example Philip Deloria, "From Nation to Neighborhood: Land, Policy, Culture, Colonialism, and Empire in U.S.–Indian Relations," *The Cultural Turn in U.S. History: Past, Present, and Future*, eds. James W. Cook, Lawrence B. Glickman and Michael O'Malley (Chicago: University of Chicago Press, 2008): 350–351.
6. See for example: Debra Loy, "Criminal Law: Equal Protection and Unequal Punishment Under the Major Crimes Act: *United States v. Cleveland*," *American Indian Law Review* 3.1 (1975): 103–108; Steven Johnson, "Jurisdiction: Criminal Jurisdiction and Enforcement Problems on Indian Reservations in the Wake of Oliphant," *American Indian Law Review* 7.2 (1979): 291–317; Taiawagi Helton and Lindsay G. Robertson, "The Foundations of Federal Indian Law and Its Application in the Twentieth Century," *Beyond Red Power: American Indian Politics and Activism Since 1900*, eds. Daniel M. Cobb and Loretta Fowler (Santa Fe: School for Advanced Research Press, 2007).
7. Ibid. See also Deborah Rosen, "Colonization Through the Law: The Judicial Defense of State Indian Legislation, 1790–1880," *The American Journal of Legal History* 46.1 (2004): 26–54.
8. Kevin Meisner, "Modern Problems of Criminal Jurisdiction in Indian Country," *American Indian Law Review* 17.1 (1992) 175–207.
9. See notes 6 and 7.
10. Amnesty International, *Maze*.
11. Available at http://thomas.loc.gov/, the Thomas database allows the user to search the Congressional record to research discourse on legislation.
12. See: Kimberlé Crenshaw, "Mapping the Margins: Intersectionality, Identity Politics, and Violence Against Women of Color," *Stanford Law Review* 43.6 (1991) 1241–1299; Patricia Hill Collins, *Black Feminist Thought, Knowledge, Consciousness, and the Politics of Empowerment* (Boston: Unwin Hyman Inc., 1991); and Chandra Talpade Mohanty, "Under Western Eyes: Feminist Scholarship and Colonial Discourses," *Third World Women and the Politics of Feminism*, eds. Chandra Mohanty, Ann Russo and Lourdes Torres (Indianapolis: University of Indiana Press, 1991).

13. Crenshaw, "Mapping the Margins."
14. See: Smith, *Conquest*; Renya Ramirez, "Race, Tribal Nation, and Gender: A Native Feminist Approach to Belonging," *Meridians: Feminism, Race, Transnationalism* 7.2 (2007) 22–40; Luana Ross, "From the 'F' Word to Indigenous/Feminisms," *Wicazo Sa Review* 24.2 (2009) 39–52.
15. Ibid.
16. Smith, *Conquest* 8; referencing the work of Neferti Tadiar.
17. See for example Deer, "Sovereignty of the Soul" and Weaver, "The Colonial Context."
18. For other scholarship on the construction of the Native woman's body see Rayna Green, "The Pocahontas Perplex: The Image of Indian Women in American Culture," *Massachusetts Review* 16.4 (1975): 698–714 and Yolanda Venegas, "The Erotics of Racialization: Gender and the Sexuality in the Making of California," *Frontiers: A Journal of Women Studies* 25.3 (2004): 63–89.
19. Smith, *Conquest.*
20. See for example: Loy, "Criminal Law."
21. Ibid. See also Kathryn A. Ritcheske, "Liability of Non-Indian Batterers in Indian Country: A Jurisdictional Analysis," *Texas Journal of Women and the Law* 14.201 (2005): 201–225.
22. See: William V. Vetter, "A New Corridor for the Maze: Tribal Criminal Jurisdiction and Nonmember Indians," *American Indian Law Review* 17.2 (1992): 444; Lisa Pisarello, "Lawless By Design: Jurisdiction, Gender and Justice in Indian Country," *Emory Law Journal* 59 (2010): 1515–1552; and Johnson, "Criminal Jurisdiction."
23. Vetter, "A New Corridor for the Maze" 444.
24. Pisarello, "Lawless By Design" 1543.
25. Ibid.
26. Vetter, "A New Corridor for the Maze."
27. Jonathan Mills and Kara Brown, "Law Enforcement in Indian Country: The Struggle for a Solution," Web. 1 Nov. 2002. <uchastings.edu/site_files/indiancountry.pdf > Accessed 12 Apr. 2011.
28. Johnson, "Criminal Jurisdiction and Enforcement Problems" 302, 315–317.
29. See for example David Castleman, "Personal Jurisdiction in Tribal Courts," *University of Pennsylvania Law Review* 154.5 (2006): 1253–1282.
30. Smith, *Conquest*; INCITE! Women of Color Against Violence, ed., *The Color of Violence: The INCITE! Anthology*, (Cambridge: South End Press, 2006); INCITE! Women of Color Against Violence, ed., *The Revolution Will Not Be Funded: Beyond the Non-Profit Industrial Complex*, (Cambridge: South End Press, 2007).

CHAPTER THREE

Historicizing Jurisdiction in Indian Country

> Renee Brewer, a victim's advocate for the Citizen Potawatomi Nation remembers a woman who had been assaulted and called the police. With the attacker still hiding in the woman's closet, four different law enforcement agencies argued on the front lawn about whose case it was. As Brewer stated, "Then you wonder why these cases are not getting prosecuted—because the United States government made it as difficult as possible for us to handle our own prosecution on our own land."
>
> —LAURA SULLIVAN[1]

When Europeans first arrived in the Americas, they were simultaneously confronted with a wealth of natural resources and the Native people who owned, occupied and managed these resources.[2] In order to justify the conquest of both the land and the people that they encountered, Europeans needed a way to legitimate the theft of resources from people with a pre-existing right to them. These first justifications came in the form of law.[3]

Using Papal Bulls (decrees from the Catholic Pope viewed as supreme law), the first Europeans in the Americas were able to legalize the colonization of Native lands and the enslavement of Native people.[4] With a legal justification for their presence secured, Europeans were able to continue to settle in the Americas, eventually forming the colonies that would become the United States. And throughout its development, the United States continued to use law to legitimate its own existence as a settler-state on Native land.[5]

The body of law that governs the relationship between Native nations and the United States of America is known as federal Indian policy. Federal Indian policy has defined and codified the legal relationship between Native people and the U.S. federal government through laws, executive orders, and Supreme Court cases.[6] Many Native legal scholars argue that while federal Indian policy may at times appear contradictory, it has always been designed to manage the problematic spaces that Native people occupy vis-à-vis the U.S. settler-state.[7] Because Native people have a pre-contact right to land, their existence has always been problematic in that it threatens American hegemony and stands in the way of complete colonization. In an attempt to remedy the "Indian problem," federal Indian policy has vacillated between policies of removal (relocating Native people "out of the way"), physical genocide (annihilating physical bodies) and assimilation (policies that use cultural genocide to assimilate Native people into the fold of American hegemony).[8]

It is against this backdrop of legal violence under colonization that we can begin to situate the emergence of jurisdictional conflicts in the prosecution of sexual violence against Native women. This chapter highlights five specific laws and policies that have directly led to the creation of modern jurisdictional conflicts in Indian country. By positioning these pieces within the trajectory of federal Indian policy, I contextualize the emergence of jurisdictional conflicts as part of a colonial narrative that seeks to divest Native people of their land, resources, and inherent sovereignty as part of managing the "Indian problem." By examining this process, I highlight additional themes that emerge from these specific laws and policies. In doing so, I theorize modern jurisdictional conflicts within a larger narrative of legal violence.

Ex Parte Crow Dog—1883: The Original Jurisdictional Conflict

On August 5, 1881, a Brulé Lakota man named Crow Dog (Kȟaŋğí Šúŋka) shot and killed Spotted Tail (Siŋté Glešká, also Brulé Lakota) on the Rosebud Indian Reservation. Crow Dog was then tried and convicted for murder by the Dakota Territorial Court and sentenced to death. However, when Crow Dog arrived for his execution, he was told that he was free to go. His conviction had been appealed to the U.S. Supreme Court in *Ex Parte Crow Dog*, who ruled unanimously that the Dakota Territorial Court had no jurisdiction over the Rosebud Indian Reservation. Because this was a crime committed by a Native person, against another Native person in Indian country, the U.S. Supreme Court vacated U.S. territorial jurisdiction and returned it to the Lakota Nation.[9] Under Lakota jurisdiction, instead of the punitive measure of death, the Lakota people called for the restoration of balance to the community. Lakota law dictated that Crow Dog care for Spotted Tail's family, which included financial and material compensation. Additionally, Crow Dog would no longer be allowed to participate in community activities.[10] Whereas Crow Dog's execution would have done nothing for the Lakota community, Lakota justice effectively addressed Crow Dog's actions while using his life to aid the family that Spotted Tail left behind.[11]

As is almost always the case, local jurisdiction and social control by communities who are most familiar with the needs of their members proved to be an effective mechanism of law and order. As historian Sidney Harring points out in the case of Crow Dog:

> Brule law was functioning and able to settle the dispute [...] It also made sound policy sense: the tribes were best able to adjudicate intertribal dispute [...] whatever the underlying reasons of the killings, the Brule Sioux were in a better position to know and judge them. They had a right to do so. That is the essence of tribal sovereignty.[12]

In addition to making sense from a policy standpoint, it was also the Lakota Nation's legal right to adjudicate the matter. By virtue of the 1868 Fort Laramie Treaty, the Lakota people had the sovereign right to exercise jurisdiction in their communities.[13] While the U.S. Supreme Court agreed, the neighboring white communities were incensed over what they perceived to be "primitive," "uncivilized" tribal justice.[14]

Ex Parte Crow Dog sparked intense outrage by white communities who saw Crow Dog as "getting away with murder."[15] Rather than understand Lakota law as one that was functioning and able to manage the dispute in a restorative way, the white community insisted on capital punishment as the only appropriate mechanism for social control. The unwillingness of the white community to incorporate a Lakota perspective into their understanding of law and order fueled intense fear of lawlessness in and around Indian country. As Native people were constructed as "savage" and "barbarous," Spotted Tail's murder and Crow Dog's subsequent release confirmed these suspicions.[16]

In addition to intense white anxiety over perceived "frontier lawlessness" in Indian country, discourse around *Ex Parte Crow Dog* demonstrates the emergence of a strong civilizing narrative in federal Indian policy. Here, Native justice systems were not only seen as dangerous to surrounding white communities, but also dangerous to Native communities themselves as they allowed savagery to triumph over civilization. As then-Secretary of the Interior Henry Teller noted of Crow Dog's case in 1883:

> [M]any of the [Indian] agencies are without law of any kind, the necessity for some role of government on the reservations grows more and more apparent each day. If it

> is the purpose of the Government [sic] to civilize the Indians, they must be compelled to desist from the savage and barbarous practices that are calculated to continue them in savagery [...][17]

Perceived notions of savagery presented a distinct problem for the federal government. At the time of *Ex Parte Crow Dog*, Indian country was seen as a lawless space that was dangerous to surrounding white communities.[18] In order to address this problem, Native people would need to be civilized. Therefore, white anxiety over Crow Dog's case was not just about fears of lawlessness, but also that the civilization of Native people, as part of remedying the so-called "Indian problem," would be disrupted if Crow Dog was to be left to "uncivilized" "tribal justice."[19] As Deloria and Lytle note:

> [...] to give compensation for a murder instead of invoking the death penalty, was considered a symbol of continued savage resistance to the overtures of a sincere "civilized" efforts to assist the Indians. All that people knew, or understood, was that the federal government was releasing rather than executing an admitted murderer.[20]

In Crow Dog's case, pervasive stereotypes of Native people and profound anxiety over lawlessness created a climate in which Native justice itself was constructed as a threat to proximate white communities and to American hegemony as a whole. As we see from Deloria and Lytle's commentary, there is a dichotomy between civilization and savagery in *Ex Parte Crow Dog* where the triumph of Lakota justice signaled a disruption in the civilizing mission of American law and policy. Within the narrative of perceived lawlessness in Crow Dog's case, a subtext emerges that integrally links the protection of non-Native bodies with a civilizing agenda. This transitory narrative in which Native people can evolve from savagery into civilization through the colonization of their governments by American law serves the dual purpose of addressing the "Indian problem" through assimilation, while also quelling white fears of perceived lawlessness in Indian country.

After *Crow Dog*, the federal government felt it had to act quickly to assuage white American fears of Indian country lawlessness while simultaneously repositioning Native peoples onto the trajectory of civilization. To accomplish these goals, Congress passed the Major Crimes Act.[21]

The Major Crimes Act—1885

Less than two years after the U.S. Supreme Court overturned Crow Dog's conviction, the Major Crimes Act was signed into law. The Major Crimes Act extends jurisdiction over certain "major" crimes committed in Indian country to the federal government.[22] If the Major Crimes Act had been passed before the murder of Spotted Tail, Crow Dog would have almost certainly been executed. Though only two paragraphs long, the Major Crimes Act is a substantial encroachment on Native sovereignty that continues to impact Native communities today. As negative ideological constructions of Native people were codified into law, the fear of Native savagery facilitated the divestment in Native self-determination that laid the foundation for contemporary jurisdictional conflicts.

Though white fear over perceived lawlessness was central to the creation of the Major Crimes Act, the impetus behind the law was also deeply paternal. As legal scholar Philip Prygoski notes of the Major Crimes Act, "The underlying theory was that tribes were not competent to deal with serious issues of crime and punishment,"[23] signaling that both Native and non-Native communities could only be adequately protected from Indian country violence by the federal government. As Wayne Ducheneaux, former President of the National Congress of American Indians remarked in a 1991 Senate subcommittee meeting:

> [O]ur method of dealing with [murder] was Crow Dog should go take care of Spotted Tail's family, and if he didn't do that we'd banish him from the tribe. But that was considered too barbaric [...] so they passed the Major Crimes Act that said we don't know how to handle murderers and they were going to show us.[24]

Ducheneaux's statement highlights the idea that Native law was read as an absence of law, and that in order for the federal government to complete its civilizing mission, it was necessary to colonize Native justice systems themselves. Ducheneaux implicates the twin narratives of paternalism and civilization present in the creation of the Major Crimes Act. Here, the Act not only "protects" white people from the perceived lawlessness of Native communities, but it also "protects" tribes from themselves. While Native justice was considered "barbaric," Western-style justice would be able to show Native nations how to properly handle major crimes, thereby aiding in their civilization.[25]

Furthermore, in protecting tribes from their own barbarity while mollifying white communities, Congress was also able to address the "Indian problem," by readying Native nations for assimilation into the body of the American politic. As scholars Carol Lujan and Gordon Adams note, the Major Crimes Act was consistent with a trend towards "policies of dependency and systematic assimilation."[26] Here, the Major Crimes Act was not just about protecting the individual interests of neighboring whites who feared Native lawlessness, but it was also about protecting the United States' vested interests in assimilating Native people in the interest of resolving the "Indian problem."

Though passed over one hundred years ago, the Major Crimes Act is still the law of the land today and continues to be one of the first major inroads into Native jurisdictional sovereignty.[27] By trumping Native jurisdiction, the Major Crimes Act overrode treaties established between many Native nations and the U.S. government that stipulated jurisdictional autonomy. For example, though the Fort Laramie Treaty of 1868 guaranteed jurisdictional authority for the Lakota people (as demonstrated in *Ex Parte Crow Dog*), the Major Crimes Act effectively abrogated this provision without the consent of Native constituents. As such, the Major Crimes Act set the stage for further encroachments into tribal sovereignty.[28]

Through its effect on tribal sovereignty, the Act laid the foundation for modern jurisdictional conflicts. The Major Crimes Act drastically affects Native jurisdiction by introducing a separate sovereign into Indian country. As a result of the Major Crimes Act, when a crime occurs, one must first determine the type of crime (major or non-major). Then a two-pronged system of jurisdictional authority must be navigated in which Native nations and the federal government may have either exclusive or dual jurisdiction over the same crime.[29] And, as the following sections will show, subsequent laws and policies have exacerbated problems stemming from the Major Crimes Act, creating additional jurisdictional complexity.

The Dawes General Allotment Act—1887

During the same legislative era as *Ex Parte Crow Dog* and the Major Crimes Act, the General Allotment Act (Dawes Act) of 1887 was passed. While not specifically targeting reservation crime or jurisdiction, the Dawes Act had dramatic and enduring effects on the racial and spatial character of Indian country. Since jurisdiction is first predicated on location, the changing composition of reservation communities under Dawes continues to have deleterious effects on the ability of tribal communities to manage the activities on their land.[30]

The same desire to assimilate Native people into "civilized" Anglo-American society that was present in the Major Crimes Act is a major component in the creation and implementation of the Dawes Act.[31] Under this Act, reservation land that was guaranteed by right of treaty to Native nations as sovereign territory was divided into individual parcels by the federal government. These parcels were then distributed to individual Indian people. Rather than having a large area on which to live communally, many Native nations were divided and individual Indian people were allotted plots of land. The size of an individual Indian's parcel was usually 160 acres, often awarded to male heads of a nuclear household.[32] As former

President Theodore Roosevelt put it, this strategy was designed as a "mighty pulverizing engine to break up the tribal mass," by replacing communal landholdings with individual ones.[33]

In an effort to remedy the "Indian problem," the Dawes Act was an assimilative effort to mold Native peoples into Euro-American farmers.[34] While the Major Crimes Act used "law and order" to "civilize" Native people, the Dawes Act used patriarchy and Euro-American gender roles. As Andrea Smith argues in *Conquest: Sexual Violence and American Indian Genocide*, land division under the Dawes Act was designed to inscribe hierarchies into non-hierarchical people in order to better control and assimilate the population as a whole.[35] If Native people could be civilized through agriculture and land privatization, the logic went, they could then be brought into the fold of white American hegemony and cease to be a cultural and financial burden on the United States. And, if Native men could be taught to control Native women under the Dawes Act (through male land ownership, patrilineal inheritance, shifting women out of the public and into the private sphere), then the U.S. could solve the "Indian problem" through dividing and conquering.[36]

While the assimilationist impulse behind the law was genuine, the desire to "civilize" Native people through the Dawes Act was a distant second to the primary goal of appropriating Native land for white settlement. As members of Congress who opposed allotment noted, "The real aim of [allotment] is to get at the Indian lands and open them up to settlement. The provisions for the apparent benefit of the Indian are but the pretext to get at his lands and occupy them."[37] Under the Dawes Act, after all individual Indian parcels were allocated, whatever land was "leftover" was conveniently freed up for the U.S. government to dispose of. This "surplus" land could then be used for railroads, extracting natural resources, and for white settlement.[38] When the Dawes Act was passed in 1887, Indian landholdings were estimated to be approximately 138 million acres. By the time the Allotment Era ended with the passage of the Indian Reorganization Act in 1934, this number had been reduced to 48 million acres—a total loss of approximately two-thirds or ninety million acres. This is an area about the size of Montana.[39]

Though the Allotment Era ended in the 1930s, the effects of the Dawes Act persist. In addition to illegally divesting Native peoples of the land guaranteed to them by treaty, the Dawes Act introduced a large population of white settlers into land previously occupied exclusively by Native nations.[40] Land that was once a large, relatively homogeneous space was divided into small parcels on which Native and non-Native families lived in close proximity. Allotments owned by Native individuals were interspersed with parcels owned by private American citizens, state governments, and the federal government. In jurisdictional terms, this "checkerboarding" made the boundary between Native and non-Native land shift from being relatively distinct to impossibly entangled.[41] Inheritance policies written into the Dawes Act exacerbate this entanglement through a phenomenon called "fractionation." Because the Dawes Act divided Native parcels equally among children upon the death of the head of household, individual parcels have subsequently gotten smaller and smaller. Today, more than 100 years after the Dawes Act became law, some individual plots have been reduced to less than one square foot of ground.[42]

The implications of the Dawes General Allotment Act in Indian country jurisdiction are profound. As jurisdiction is predicated on the location of a crime, the Dawes Act has made determining whether a parcel in Indian country is governed by tribal, state, or federal entities exceptionally complex. Additionally, the inundation of Indian country with non-Native residents has complicated matters further, as increased interactions between white Americans and Native people form the foundation of subsequent federal Indian policy that challenges Native jurisdictional sovereignty.

Public Law 280–1953

Though policies of outright physical annihilation of Native peoples were abandoned by the middle of the twentieth-century, the U.S. federal government was still deeply entrenched in addressing what it continued to see as the "Indian problem." In exchange for vast tracts of land, the federal government entered into what is known as a "trust relationship" with Native peoples. Under the trust relationship, the federal government became the trustee of Native resources and, in exchange, guaranteed that it would provide vital services to Indian country and protect Native land and sovereignty.[43] While the federal government enjoyed the economic resources it acquired through treaties, by the 1950s it was reluctant to use any of these resources to make good on its responsibilities to Native people.[44] Under the trust relationship, the "Indian problem" endured as Native people stood in the way of complete American hegemony. In an effort to "solve" this "problem" Congress entered into what historians have dubbed the "Termination Era."

Starting in the late 1940s, Congress used federal Indian policy to "terminate" the relationship between the federal government and Native people to "get out of the Indian business."[45] To accomplish this, Congress ignored its own policies that recognized the sovereignty of Native people and the rights that they maintained through treaties, and began to sever the trust relationship, reduce funding to Indian country, revoke federal recognition of Indian tribes, and relocate Native people to urban areas.[46] It is in this context that Congress created Public Law 280.[47]

Public Law 280 (PL 280) was a driving force in Termination Era policies. According to Deloria and Lytle, the goal of PL 280 was "terminating federal supervision over Indians and their property with the ultimate goals of assimilating them into American society and eliminating the reservation enclaves of Indian culture."[48] Central to this goal was the massive restructuring of criminal jurisdiction in Indian country. Without the consent of tribes or states, PL 280 transferred criminal jurisdiction in Indian country to state governments in six mandatory states: California, Minnesota (except the Red Lake Nation), Nebraska, Oregon (except the Warm Springs Reservation), Wisconsin (except later the Menominee Indian Reservation) and, upon its statehood, Alaska.[49] Although only six states were mandatory PL 280 states, these six states contained 359 of the over 550 federally recognized tribes at the time, affecting over 65% of Native nations.[50] Other states in addition to the mandatory PL 280 states were allowed to opt-in to the system, and since then Nevada, South Dakota, Washington, Florida, Idaho, Montana, North Dakota, Arizona, Iowa and Utah have adopted PL 280.[51] While previous legal statutes had guaranteed Native nations freedom from state jurisdiction,[52] Public Law 280—in its quest to dissolve the federal relationship with Native nations—ignored this and granted states sweeping criminal jurisdiction in Indian country.

Though financial motivations to dissolve federal relationships with Native nations were driving forces behind the law, PL 280 reveals familiar themes of lawlessness as central to its formation. After the Dawes Act ushered in large communities of white settlers in and around Indian country, the new non-Native residents were quick to express profound anxiety over the activities in Indian country, describing Native people as "disorderly and incapable of self-government"[53] and Indian country as places of "rampant crime and disorder."[54] Native justice systems were again constructed as weak and ineffective, while federal jurisdiction was considered distant and limited.[55] While the Major Crimes Act had intended to address concerns of lawlessness in Indian country, transferring jurisdiction to the federal government had merely created a system in which a distant and unresponsive federal government had failed to address law and order at all.[56] This was exacerbated by Termination Era policies that severely cut vital services to Native nations, impeding Native communities from maintaining law and order through the limited jurisdictional authority that they still maintained. Ironically the result was that the very system that had sought to address fears of lawlessness had, in reality, created a very real sense of lawlessness in Indian country.[57]

To address the reality of lawlessness that emerged as the result of its own policies, some scholars note that the federal government could have addressed the issue by strengthening tribal justice systems.[58] Native nations had always had fully functioning systems of law and order, and it wasn't until this system was disrupted that a true sense of lawlessness began to emerge.[59] However, funding Native nations did not fit with an assimilationist paradigm and was especially incongruent with Termination Era policies of dissolving federal relationships with tribes. Instead, the federal government decided to legislate over the problem by passing PL 280 and farming out federal jurisdiction to state agencies. This accomplished several goals of the Termination Era project: it saved the federal government money as it took steps to "get out of the Indian business," it severed federal relationships with Native nations, and it quieted white anxiety over perceived lawlessness by transferring jurisdiction to state authorities.[60]

While Congress acted ostensibly to address white fears of lawlessness, it was readily apparent that dissolving its financial responsibility to Native nations was more important than addressing concerns over law and order in earnest. As one publication put it, "Congress was concerned about satisfying the law and order demands of Anglos living on or near reservations, but only so long as the federal government did not have to pay."[61] The transfer of jurisdiction to state governments under PL 280 turned out to be an unfunded mandate. Under PL 280, state governments were forced to manage crime on reservations, yet did not receive any additional funding to do so. With no funding from the federal government, and with no tax revenues generated from reservations within their boundaries, state governments were reluctant to use any of their resources on law enforcement in Indian country. This had major consequences as Native infrastructure weakened and state governments refused to fill any law enforcement shortfalls. As Goldberg and Champagne note:

> Public Law 280 was supposed to provide the solution to the problem of "lawlessness" by empowering state civil and criminal courts to do what the tribal and federal systems supposedly could not. Ironically and tragically, however, Public Law 280 has itself become the source of lawlessness on reservations.[62]

Called "one of the most bold and discriminating actions against Natives in the legal and judicial system,"[63] PL 280 had devastating effects on Native nations, which continue to manifest today. As an unfunded mandate, state law enforcement in Indian country has become sporadic.[64] As a divestment in tribal sovereignty, Native nations have been unable to exercise local control over the activities in their own community.[65] While this contributes to an overall sense of lawlessness in general, PL 280 also contributes to the creation and maintenance of modern jurisdictional conflicts in particular.[66]

In an attempt to terminate federal responsibility over Native people, PL 280 introduced a third sovereign into the jurisdictional schema in Indian country. While the Major Crimes Act introduced the federal government as a second sovereign (sometimes competing with and sometimes usurping tribal jurisdiction), under PL 280, state governments became a third entity with which to negotiate jurisdiction. While these complications make crime in Indian country more difficult to adjudicate in general, it has a disproportionate impact on Native women, as cases of sexual assault often fall through the cracks.[67]

Oliphant v. Suquamish Indian Tribe—1978

As a direct result of Allotment Era policies, the Port Madison Indian Reservation located in northwest Washington is home to a large number of non-Native residents. By the 1970s, approximately 63% of the reservation was owned by non-Native individuals, living alongside Native families on a checkerboard of individual parcels.[68]

In August 1973, Mark David Oliphant, a non-Native resident, allegedly assaulted a Suquamish tribal police officer and resisted arrest. Oliphant was arrested and charged by tribal police.[69] Though Oliphant is a non-Native person, treaties with Native nations have consistently recognized Native jurisdiction over non-Native perpetrators. This jurisdictional language was often repeated in treaties with various tribes. For example Article V of the 1785 Treaty of Hopewell with the Cherokee states:

> If any citizen of the United States, or other person not being an Indian, shall attempt to settle on any of the lands [...] which are hereby allotted to the Indians [...] such persons shall forfeit the protection of the United States, and the Indians may punish him or not as they please.[70]

After his arrest, Oliphant appealed his case to local courts who rejected it, citing the inherent sovereignty of the Suquamish to maintain law and order within their communities.[71] This was in accordance with previous case law, as well as with treaties signed by other tribes. Oliphant then appealed this decision to the U.S. Supreme Court in *Oliphant v. Suquamish Indian Tribe*, and on March 6, 1978, the Supreme Court reversed the lower court's decision. Ruling that Native nations do not have the legal right to arrest and prosecute non-Native offenders, the court sided in favor of Oliphant in a six to two decision.[72]

The Oliphant decision colonized the inherent (and dually codified) right of pre-constitutional Native nations to govern the people and activities on their own land, and was thus a devastating blow to tribal sovereignty.[73] Under *Oliphant*, Native nations were prohibited from exercising jurisdiction over non-Native individuals on Indian land. While the authority to maintain local control within a society is central to maintaining law and order, the Oliphant decision denies Native communities this basic tenet of self-determination. As Lujan and Adams note, "Oliphant strikes directly at the heart of a tribe's ability to protect itself by institutionalizing discourses that deny tribal police the protection and authority that every other community in America bestows on their police."[74]

The background and discourse around the Oliphant case reveals familiar themes of racism and paternalism. At the time of Oliphant's arrest, the Suquamish had a fully functioning Western-style court system. Yet, as a white American, Oliphant was relieved of his responsibility as a Suquamish community member. Despite the fact that the Suquamish had "elevated" themselves to the level of American judicial hegemony, the federal government viewed them as somehow short of truly entering American civilization. The outcome of *Oliphant* indicates that even the "civilizing" project of previous federal Indian policy was not enough to trump the enduring myth of Native savagery, and begs the question: what, if anything, can?[75]

Paired with the myth of Native savagery, white anxiety over Native lawlessness endures in *Oliphant*. In the majority opinion, Justice William Rehnquist cited a previous case, *In re Mayfield* to justify his ruling against the Suquamish:

> In *In re Mayfield* (1891) the Court noted that the policy of Congress had been to allow the inhabitants of the Indian country "such power of self-government as was thought to be consistent with the safety of the white population with which they may have come in contact, and to encourage them as far as possible in raising themselves to our standard of civilization."[76]

In *In re Mayfield*, white fears of the perceived violence and danger of Native communities were enmeshed with the civilizing mission inherent to the assimilationist paradigm of federal Indian policy. *Mayfield* indicates that divesting Native nations of their inherent and pre-existing sovereign right to exercise jurisdiction in their own communities served a dual purpose: it protected white bodies, while also delivering Native people into civilization. Rehnquist's decision to use the racist language of *In re Mayfield* in *Oliphant* reflects this—his argument essentially being that since the U.S. Supreme Court has already acted in favor of protecting white interests and "civilizing" Native nations, that the current court must follow suit. Despite noting in *Oliphant* that "Congress never expressly forbade Indian tribes to impose criminal penalties on non-Indians,"[77] Rehnquist still insisted on leveraging

the power of the U.S. Supreme Court to effectively do so. Here, Rehnquist chose to engage with the vague and racist statute set in *In re Mayfield*, rather than uphold tribal sovereignty which had been clearly expressed in the form of many constitutionally binding treaties.

The Oliphant decision is one of the most significant blows to tribal sovereignty in American history and is a major factor in the development of modern jurisdictional conflicts. As one scholar notes, "Today, thanks to *Oliphant*, non-Indians know that practically no one has criminal jurisdiction over them on the Indian reservations,"[78] creating a climate in which violence against Native people is often met with impunity. Like PL 280, *Oliphant* illustrates the colonial irony that the *fear* of lawlessness by white communities creates a very *real* sense of lawlessness for Native people in Indian country.

Conclusion

The epigraph at the beginning of this chapter tells of a victim's advocate recounting a night when four different law enforcement officers chose to argue over jurisdiction rather than confront the perpetrator or address the needs of the survivor. The advocate states, "Then you wonder why these cases are not getting prosecuted—because the United States government made it as difficult as possible for us to handle our own prosecution on our own land."

This chapter argues that the U.S. government has, indeed, made it as difficult as possible for Native people to manage their own prosecutions on their own land. Though control over the activity on one's land is fundamental to community safety, the U.S. federal government has consistently encroached upon this sovereign right, transforming law and order in Indian country from something that was once local and efficient, to one that is distant and largely ineffective. While some legal scholars treat jurisdictional conflicts as collateral damage from a complicated yet necessary system needed to address the "unique" legal relationship between the federal government and Native nations,[79] I have demonstrated that this is not the case. Instead, jurisdictional conflicts are the direct result of federal Indian policy that has consistently used legal violence as a method to colonize Native land, assimilate Native people, and "solve" the "Indian problem."

Additionally, a closer examination of these five pieces of law and policy reveals more subtle themes. *Ex Parte Crow Dog*, the Major Crimes Act, the Dawes General Allotment Act, Public Law 280, and *Oliphant v. Suquamish Indian Tribe* each demonstrate that the policies most directly responsible for the creation of modern jurisdictional conflicts are also marked by paternalism, a civilizing mission,

investment in white American hegemony, protection of white bodies from the perceived threat of Native savagery, the protection of white economic and social interests, divestments in tribal sovereignty, and the colonization of Native justice systems. In turn, it becomes impossible to separate the motivations behind these policies from their results, as jurisdictional conflicts *themselves* emerge as marked by these themes. Thus, when four law enforcement agencies argue on the front lawn of a Native woman's home as her attacker remains hidden in the closet, hundreds of years of federal policy are inscribing legal violence on her and her community. Paternalism, divestments in tribal sovereignty, and investments in white American hegemony are literally part of the violation that this woman experiences as her attack is met with impunity. Jurisdictional conflicts, the history of federal Indian policy, and legal violence can therefore not be separated. While this affects all Native people in Indian communities, this type of legal violence often affects Native women in particular. The next chapter illustrates the way these laws shape the experience of Native women in Indian country, arguing that sexual violence against Native women today is structured by this history of legal violence against Native communities as a whole.

Notes

1. Laura Sullivan, "Legal Hurdles Stall Rape Cases on Native Lands," *National Public Radio* 26 Jul. 2007.
2. Barbara Perry, *Policing Race and Place in Indian Country: Over and Underenforcement* (New York: Lexington Books, 2009): 35.
3. Robert Williams, *The American Indian in Western Legal Thought: The Discourses of Conquest* (New York: Oxford University Press: 1990) 6–8.
4. Ibid. See also Wilcomb E. Washburn, *Red Man's Land/White Man's Law: The Past and Present Status of the American Indian* 2nd Edition. (Norman: University of Oklahoma Press, 1971) 5.
5. Ibid.
6. Steven Pevar, *The Rights of Indians and Tribes: The Authoritative ACLU Guide to Indian Tribal Rights* (Carbondale: Southern Illinois University Press, 1992) 4.
7. See for example: John Vinzant, "A Brief History of Federal Indian Policy." *The Supreme Court's Role in American Indian Policy.* 2009.
8. Helton and Robertson, "Foundations of Federal Indian Law."
9. Sidney L. Harring, *Crow Dog's Case: American Indian Sovereignty Tribal Law, and United States Law in the Nineteenth Century* (Cambridge: Cambridge University Press, 1994) 129–141.
10. Mary Crow Dog, *Lakota Woman* (New York: Harper Perennial, 1990) 183.
11. Steve Russell, "Making Peace With Crow Dog's Ghost: Racialized Prosecution in Federal Indian Law," *Wicazo Sa Review* (Spring 2006): 61.

12. Sidney Harring, "Crow Dog and the Western Justice System," *Tribal Criminal Law and Procedure*, eds. Sarah Deer and Carrie E. Garrow (New York: Altamira Press, 2007) 50.
13. Ibid.
14. Perry, *Policing Race and Place* 36.
15. Deloria and Lytle, *American Indians, American Justice* 169–170.
16. Perry, *Policing Race and Place* 36.
17. As quoted in Perry *Policing Race and Place* 36.
18. Thomas Biolsi, "Imagined Geographies: Sovereignty, Indigenous Space, and American Indian Struggle," *American Ethnologist* 32.2 (2005): 244.
19. Perry, *Policing Race and Place* 36.
20. Deloria and Lytle, *American Indians, American Justice* 169–170.
21. Eileen Luna-Firebaugh, *Tribal Policing: Asserting Sovereignty, Seeking Justice,* (Tucson: University of Arizona Press, 2007) 33; Pevar, *The Rights of Indians and Tribes* 78.
22. When first passed, the Major Crimes Act included "major" crimes such as murder, manslaughter, kidnapping and rape. Since its passage, the Major Crimes Act was amended to include many other felony crimes including robbery, incest, sexual abuse of a minor, and assault with a deadly weapon (Pevar, *The Rights of Indians and Tribes* 144–145).
23. Philip J. Prygoski, "From Marshall to Marshall: The Supreme Court's Changing Stance on Tribal Sovereignty," *American Bar Association* (Fall 1995): 2.
24. "Indian Civil Rights Act": Hearing Before the Select Committee on Indian Affairs, 102nd Cong. 42 (1991) as quoted in Pisarello, "Lawless By Design" 1515.
25. Sarah Deer and Carrie E. Garrow, eds. *Tribal Criminal Law and Procedure*. (New York: Altamira Press, 2007) 45.
26. Carol Lujan and Gordon Adams, "U.S. Colonization of Indian Justice Systems: A Brief History," *Wicazo Sa Review* 19.2 (2004) 16.
27. "Sexual Assault in Indian Country: Confronting Sexual Violence," *National Sexual Violence Resource Center*. Web. (2000): 6. <http://www.nsvrc.org/_cms/fileUpload/indian.htm> Accessed 12 Apr. 2011. (Quoting the work of Sarah Deer, draft document prepared in support of changes to federal legislation, University of Kansas, School of Law, 1997).
28. Deer, "Sovereignty of the Soul."
29. Garrow and Deer, *Tribal Criminal Law* 93–94.
30. Lujan and Adams, "U.S. Colonization of Indian Justice" 16.
31. Biolsi, "Imagined Geographies" 244.
32. Pevar, *The Rights of Indians and Tribes* 8–9.
33. Kevin Bruyneel, *The Third Space of Sovereignty: The Postcolonial Politics of U.S.-Indigenous Relations* (Minnesota: University of Minnesota Press, 2007) 94.
34. Biolsi, "Imagined Geographies" 244.
35. Smith, *Conquest.*
36. Ibid.; Mihesuah, *Indigenous American Women*.
37. "Lands in Severalty to Indians: Views of the Minority." *Index to the Reports of Committees of the House of Representatives for the First and Second Sessions of the Forty-Sixth Congress 1879–1880.* Volume 5—Nos. 1521–1793. Washington, D.C.: Government Printing Office, 1880: 10.
38. Pevar, *The Rights of Indians and Tribes* 70, 99, 121–122.

39. Charles F. Wilkinson and Christine L. Miklas, *Indian Tribes As Sovereign Governments: A Sourcebook on Federal-Tribal History, Law and Policy* (Oakland: AIRI, 1988) 9–10.
40. Larson, "Making Sense of Federal Indian Law" 14.
41. Ibid., 20.
42. 1922 report from the General Accounting Office, cited by Brian Sawers, "Tribal Land Corporations: Using Incorporation to Combat Fractionation," *Nebraska Law Review* 88.2 (2009): 398.
43. Pevar, *The Rights of Indians and Tribes* 32–41.
44. Vanessa J. Jimenez and Soo C. Song, "Concurrent Tribal and State Jurisdiction Under Public Law 280," *American University Law Review* 47.1627 (1998).
45. Luana Ross, *Inventing the Savage* (Austin: University of Texas Press, 1998) 24.
46. Ibid.
47. Frank Pommersheim, *Braid of Feathers: American Indian Law and Contemporary Tribal Life* (Berkeley: University of California Press, 1997) 122.
48. Deloria and Lytle, *American Indians, American Justice* 175.
49. Pevar, *The Rights of Indians and Tribes* 123–125.
50. Jimenez and Song, "Concurrent Tribal and State Jurisdiction" 1634.
51. Ibid.
52. *Worcester v. Georgia* (1832). For a discussion of this case see Joanne Barker, "For Whom Sovereignty Matters" *Sovereignty Matters*, ed. Joanne Barker (Lincoln: University of Nebraska Press, 2005): 6–11.
53. Carole E. Goldberg, "Public Law 280," *American Indian Treaties Publication* (Los Angeles: University of California, Los Angeles American Indian Culture and Research Center. Series No. 1, 1975) 4.
54. Goldberg and Champagne 1996, referenced in Sarah Deer, "Federal Indian Law and Violent Crime: Native Women and Children at the Mercy of the State," *The Color of Violence* 35.
55. Ross, *Inventing the Savage* 24.
56. Luna-Firebaugh, *Tribal Policing* 25.
57. Deer, "Federal Indian Law and Violent Crime" 35.
58. Pommersheim, *Braid of Feathers* 122.
59. Ibid.
60. Luna-Firebaugh, *Tribal Policing* 117.
61. Goldberg, "Public Law 280" 3.
62. Quoted in Deer, "Federal Indian Law and Violent Crime" 35.
63. Ross, *Inventing the Savage* 24.
64. Deloria and Lytle, *American Indians, American Justice* 176.
65. Deer, "Sovereignty of the Soul" 462.
66. Luna-Firebaugh, *Tribal Policing* 25.
67. This will be explored at length in Chapter Four.
68. *Oliphant v. Suquamish Indian Tribe.* 435 U.S. 191. U.S. Supreme Court, 1978.
69. Ibid.

70. Treaty of Hopewell as quoted in Kevin Meisner, "Modern Problems" 190. See also Article V of the 1785 Treaty with the Wyandot, Delaware and Others and Article IV of the 1830 Treaty with the Choctaw.
71. Bruce Duthu, *American Indians and the Law* (New York: Penguin Group, 2008) 19–20.
72. *Oliphant v. Suquamish.*
73. Luna-Firebaugh, *Tribal Policing* 31.
74. Lujan and Adams, "U.S. Colonization of Indian Justice" 19.
75. Please note that I am in no way encouraging the adoption of Western systems of government in Native communities. I am only using this example to demonstrate that even when Native nations complete the civilizing mission of American legal hegemony, they are still denied legitimacy as a governing body. For more on this, see my discussion of VAWA 2013 in Chapter Six.
76. *Oliphant v. Suquamish* 115–116.
77. Ibid.
78. Meisner, "Modern Problems" 206.
79. See for example Loy, "Criminal Law."

CHAPTER FOUR

Jurisdiction and Sexual Violence Against Native Women

> It's rape tourism, right here in Oklahoma, South Dakota, Alaska, and any place where the confusing mess of jurisdictional issues allow perpetrators to hide. Are there even words to describe this evil?
>
> —ANDY TERNAY[1]

Chapter Three demonstrates that legal violence has been used as a colonial tool to "solve" the social, political, legal, and physical aspects of the "Indian problem." However, to give the impression that law has been the *principal* tool of colonization would be incorrect. In fact, just as legal violence was present at first contact, so too was sexual violence against Native women.[2] While federal law constructed Native communities as unfit for political sovereignty, social constructions of Native women by colonizers portrayed Native women as having no right to corporal sovereignty.[3] By using sexual violence as a weapon, colonizers attempted to control Native nations as a whole by targeting Native women in particular. In this context, both sexual and legal violence became fused in a comprehensive colonial approach to address the problematic space that Native communities have always occupied vis-à-vis the American settler-state.

By reading sexual violence in tandem with law, I argue that non-Native criminal impunity in Indian country is not simply collateral damage from a legal system that by nature must be complex. Instead, I demonstrate the ways that modern jurisdictional conflicts are the direct result of federal policy that has *always* been characterized by both legal and sexual violence against Native people. In this chapter, I theorize sexual violence in a colonial-legal context, while demonstrating the real effects that jurisdiction has on contemporary Native women. By highlighting the way that jurisdictional conflicts disproportionately affect Native women by allowing impunity for sexual assault, I support my thesis that the confluence of legal and sexual violence present since European contact continues to maintain and inscribe colonial violence on the bodies of Native women in Indian country today.

Determining Jurisdiction in Indian Country

Regardless of her racial identity, when a woman is sexually assaulted outside of Indian country, jurisdiction is relatively straightforward. If it happens on state land, for example, it generally falls under state jurisdiction and goes to a district court (see Figure 1).[4] When a woman is sexually assaulted in Indian country however, the jurisdictional scheme is quite different. In Indian country—because of the Major Crimes Act, Public Law 280, *Oliphant*, and recently the Violence Against Women Reauthorization Act of 2013—the type of crime, exactly where it occurred, the racial identity of the perpetrator and victim, and the nature of their relationship to each other and to the community all play key roles in determining jurisdictional authority.[5]

Because of the Major Crimes Act, when a crime is committed in Indian country, the type of crime (major or non-major) must be determined. Sexual assault is always considered a "major" crime and the Major Crimes Act applies.[6] Here, the Major Crimes Act immediately introduces a second sovereign in addition to the Native nation. While non-major crimes may fall under the sole jurisdiction of the tribe, major crimes introduce either the state or the federal government as a second sovereign that may have either sole jurisdiction over the crime or may share jurisdiction with the tribe. In cases of dual jurisdiction, double jeopardy does not attach because the crime falls under the jurisdiction of separate sovereigns.[7] To determine which second sovereign (the state or the federal government) is introduced under the Major Crimes Act, it is vital to determine exactly where the crime occurred.

If it is determined that all or part of a crime was committed in Indian country, it must then be determined whether or not the land on which the crime was committed is subject to Public Law 280 (PL 280). If it is determined that the assault occurred in Indian country subject to state jurisdiction under PL 280, then the Major Crimes Act introduces that state as a second sovereign. In these cases, depending on the racial identity of the parties involved and the nature of their relationship to each other and to the Native community, the state either maintains sole jurisdiction over the crime or dual jurisdiction shared with the tribe. If it is determined that the assault occurred on land not subject to PL 280, then the second sovereign introduced by the Major Crimes Act is the federal government. Then, depending on the racial identity of the parties involved and the nature of their relationship to each other and to the Native community, the federal government either maintains sole jurisdiction over the crime or dual jurisdiction shared with the tribe.[8]

Determining PL 280 status is often difficult. While the 1953 law initially forced the transfer of federal jurisdiction to six mandatory states, subsequently other states have been allowed to opt in and out of PL 280 status.[9] Some Native nations were once under PL 280 jurisdiction but retroceded from it, creating exceptions to state jurisdiction under PL 280 in some cases. This is the case in the Umatilla Reservation in Oregon, for example, that was once under PL 280, but has since retroceded Oregon state jurisdiction.[10] Also, many states have only limited jurisdiction under PL 280. This means that a state could technically be a PL 280 state, but only have jurisdiction over air and water pollution and no jurisdiction over sexual assault (as is the case in Arizona). Or, a state might have PL 280 jurisdiction over sexual assault, but only if it occurs on highways (as is the case in South Dakota). Alternatively, a PL 280 state might have jurisdiction over civil cases, but not criminal cases (as is the case in Iowa), in which a civil suit against a rapist would fall under state jurisdiction, but a criminal case would not.[11]

Additionally, some reservations are not entirely within the bounds of a given state, sometimes crossing between PL 280 and non-PL 280 states, and even crossing between national borders. Such is the case of the Navajo Nation that spans Arizona, New Mexico and Utah, and the Mohawk Nation of Akwesasne that falls within New York in the United States and the provinces of Ontario and Quebec in Canada. Because of numerous variations and exceptions, determining if state jurisdiction under PL 280 applies can be very complicated.[12]

Yet another difficulty in determining jurisdiction comes from the Dawes Act. The division of Native land under the Dawes Act not only introduced a large white population into Indian country, but also created a checkerboard pattern of land ownership. This process of "checkerboarding" means that the boundaries of Indian country often encompass many tracts of land that are not legally part of Indian country. Because of checkerboarding, even if a survivor knows exactly where she was assaulted within the bounds of a reservation, it is often extremely difficult to find out if that particular parcel of land is technically part of Indian country.[13] As one assistant U.S. attorney remarked, "If it's a parcel of property in a rural area, it may take weeks or months to determine if it's Indian land or not;

investigators usually cannot determine this, they need attorneys to do it by going through court and title records to make a determination."[14]

These difficulties are exacerbated for crimes where the survivor is unable to determine exactly where the assault took place. In cases in which women are blindfolded, drugged, intoxicated, knocked unconscious, and/or transported in moving vehicles, mapping the exact place(s) where the assault occurred can be nearly impossible. Such was the case for two Native women in Oklahoma in 2005:

> In both cases, the women were raped by three non-Native men [...] Because the women were blindfolded, support workers were concerned that the women would be unable to say whether the rapes took place on federal, state, or tribal land. There was concern that, because of the jurisdictional complexities in Oklahoma, uncertainty about exactly where these crimes took place might affect the ability of these women to obtain justice.[15]

Compounding the difficulty of using location as a determinant in Indian country are the identity politics at work in the wake of the Oliphant decision. After the U.S. Supreme Court stripped Native nations of their ability to arrest and prosecute non-Native perpetrators in *Oliphant v. Suquamish*, the racial identities of the parties involved in Indian country crime have become central to determining jurisdiction. Once the type of crime, the location of the crime, and the applicability of PL 280 are determined, the racial identity of the parties involved must be verified to determine jurisdiction.[16] If the perpetrator is non-Native, the victim is Native, and it is determined that the crime occurred in Indian country subject to PL 280, then the state has jurisdiction. If the perpetrator is non-Native, the victim is Native, and it is determined that the assault occurred in Indian country not subject to PL 280, then the federal government has jurisdiction. If both the perpetrator and the victim are non-Native, the state has jurisdiction regardless of PL 280 status. If the assault occurs in Indian country subject to PL 280, the perpetrator is Native, and the victim is Native, then both the state and the Native nation in which it occurred have concurrent jurisdiction. If the assault occurred in Indian country not subject to PL 280 and both the perpetrator and victim are Native, then both the federal government and the Native nation in which the crime occurred have concurrent jurisdiction (see Figures 2–6).[17] Each scenario is also shaped by the relationship between the perpetrator/victim and the perpetrator/Native nation in that in some cases the tribe may extend limited jurisdiction over non-Native perpetrators under Title IX of the Violence Against Women Reauthorization Act of 2013 (VAWA 2013) when it otherwise would not.

While determining the exact location of an assault and PL 280 applicability can be incredibly difficult, determining the racial identity of those involved can be equally problematic. Despite making sweeping regulations governing the authority to manage crimes that involve "Indians" and "non-Indians," both Congress and the U.S. Supreme Court have failed to provide a consistent definition of who an "Indian" is. In fact, there are dozens of different definitions of the term "Indian" under the law.[18] As Pevar notes:

> Each government—tribal, state, and federal—decides who an Indian is for the purposes of that government's laws and programs. This can result in someone being an Indian under tribal law but not under federal law, under federal but not tribal law, under tribal but not state law, and so forth.[19]

Native identity in the United States is complicated and is often found at the confluence of racial, social, ethnic, and political elements. Often, Indian identity is not simply a matter of blood quantum or enrollment, but also a complex matrix of representation, recognition and active participation[20] that is variously recognized by tribal, state and federal governments. Based on physical appearance, someone may be labeled as "White" or "Black" but may also be an enrolled member of a Native nation. Phenotypically, someone may appear to be Native but have no Native ancestry. Alternatively, someone might be of Yaqui or Tohono O'odham ancestry but was born on the Mexican side of their ancestral homelands, rendering them "non-Indian" in the eyes of the federal government. Similarly, someone might be enrolled in a Native tribe that is not federally recognized, possibly making them "Indian" for the purposes of a state government but not the federal government. Determining Native identity may take a serious investment in not only researching legal enrollment but also in talking to individuals, community members, as well as researching family and oral history. Despite this, law enforcement officials are required to determine the Indian/non-Indian racial identity of the parties involved in a crime in order to adjudicate it.

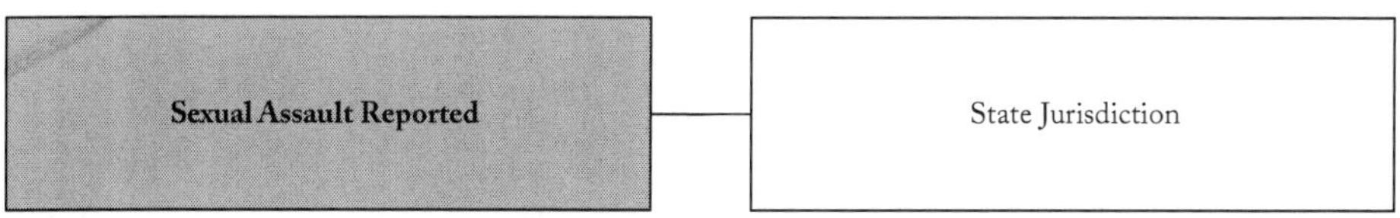

Figure 1. Jurisdiction for Sexual Assault on State Land.[21, 22]

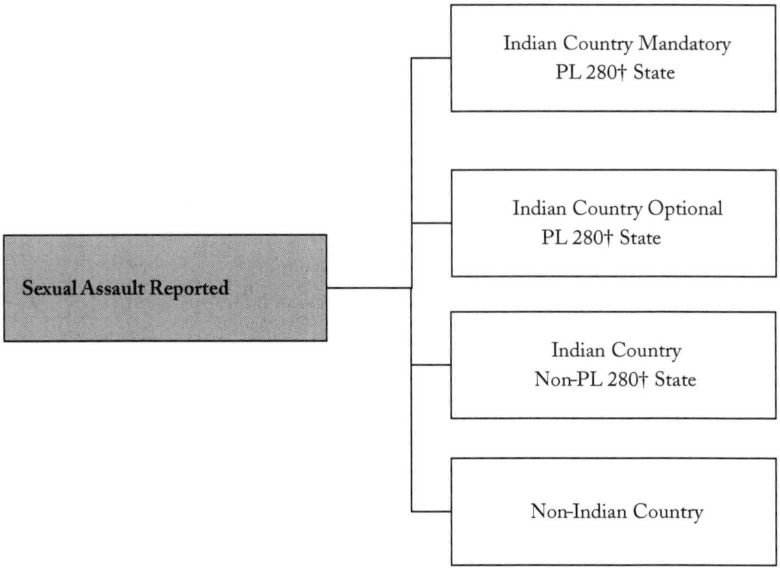

Figure 2. Types of Land In or Near Indian Country Used to Determine Jurisdiction.

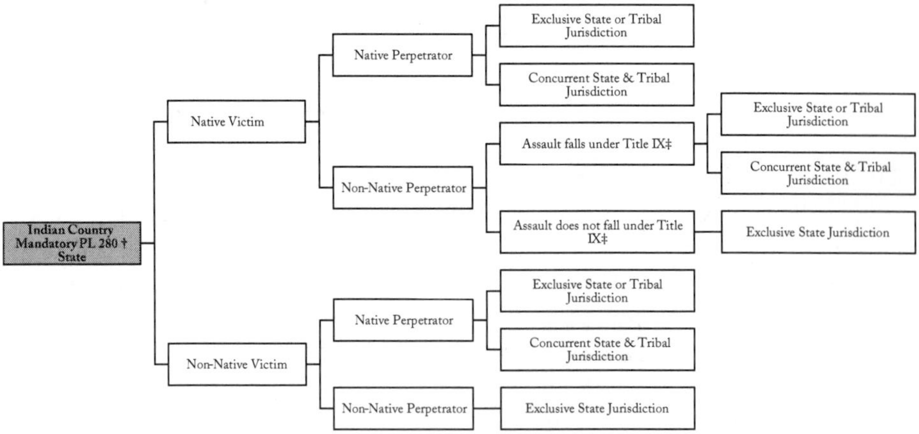

Figure 3. Jurisdiction for Sexual Assault In Indian Country, Mandatory PL 280† State.

† "PL 280" is Public Law 280.

‡ "Title IX" refers to crimes that qualify for special domestic violence jurisdiction under Title IX of the Violence Against Women Reauthorization Act of 2013.

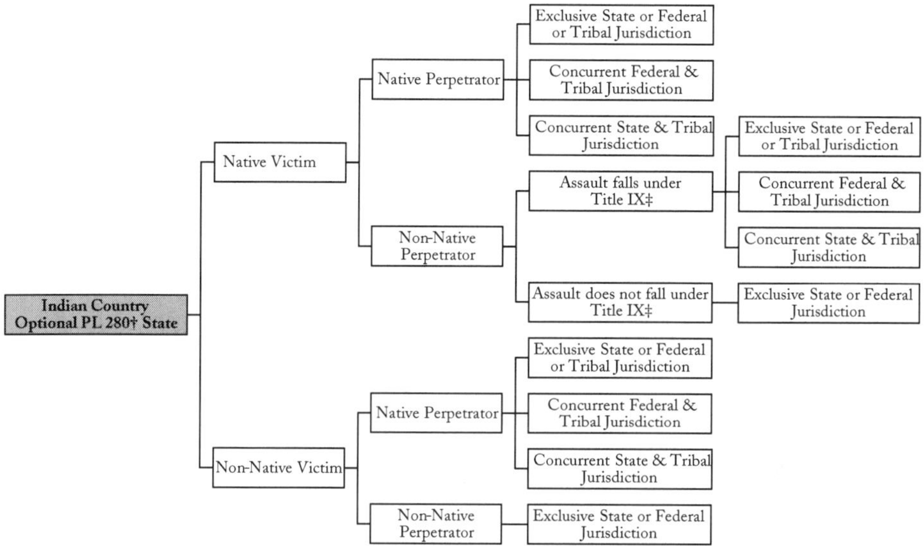

Figure 4. Jurisdiction for Sexual Assault In Indian Country, Optional PL 280† State.

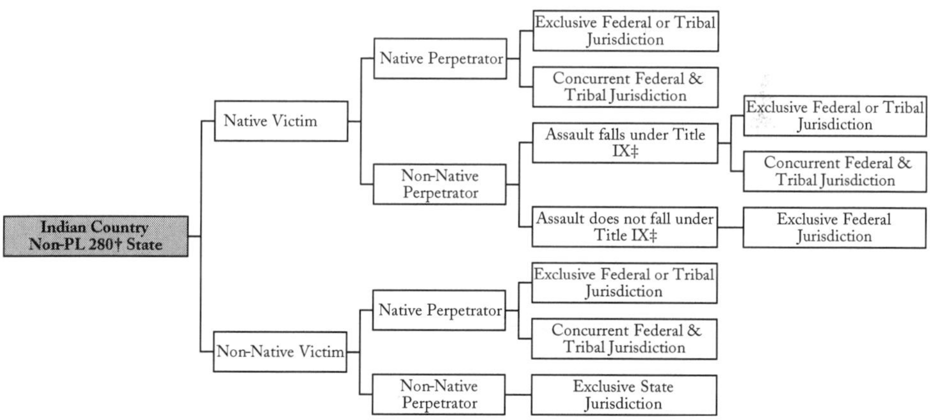

Figure 5. Jurisdiction for Sexual Assault In Indian Country, Non PL-280† State.

† "PL 280" is Public Law 280.

‡ "Title IX" refers to crimes that qualify for special domestic violence jurisdiction under Title IX of the Violence Against Women Reauthorization Act of 2013.

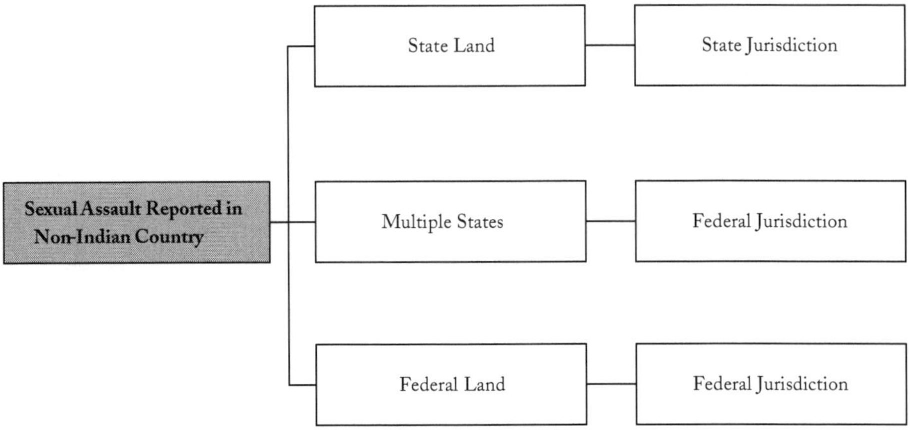

Figure 6. Jurisdiction for Sexual Assault In Non-Indian Country.[23]

Using racial identity as a criterion for arrest and prosecution is a significantly flawed approach to adjudicating crime. In addition to subjecting law enforcement officials to the complex task of determining a racial identity that is not clearly defined, using race as a jurisdictional determinant further marginalizes Native communities by collapsing ethnic identities while giving perpetrators another avenue to manipulate the criminal justice system.

The confusion created when ethnic and racial identities are enmeshed is readily apparent in the 1990 U.S. Supreme Court case *Duro v. Reina* in which Albert Duro of the Torres Martinez Desert Cahuilla Indians was accused of killing a teenage boy in the Salt River Pima Maricopa Indian Community. Here, Duro was clearly an "Indian" yet was not a member of the Native nation in which he committed the crime. This created confusion as it raised the question of whether or not non-member Indians were considered "Indians" for the purposes of jurisdiction.[24] In response, Congress passed the "Duro Fix," which provided that for the purposes of jurisdiction, all Native people—regardless of Native membership—share legal standing as "Indians" for the purposes of prosecution in Indian country.[25]

Considering that each Native nation has its own culture, history, laws and government, folding unique ethnic identities into a monolithic "Indian" racial identity is marginalizing for Native communities. On one hand, the collapse of ethnic identity is paradoxical in a jurisdictional scheme that clearly values the identity of perpetrators; on the other, it is predictable given the history of federal Indian policy. As noted in the previous chapter, federal Indian policy has been designed to protect the civilized "Us" from the savage "Other." The "Other" in this case was all "Indian" people whose savagery was defined simply by failing to be

Euro-American. Though each Native community is unique, they all became the "Indian" "Other" in the eyes of the federal government under the Duro Fix.

Using race as a jurisdictional determinate is additionally problematic when perpetrators use identity politics to avoid arrest. In some cases, suspects have exploited *Oliphant* and the Duro Fix by strategically enrolling or disenrolling themselves from their Native nations to manipulate jurisdiction and sidestep prosecution.[26] The idea that someone can be an Indian while committing a crime, and somehow be a non-Indian while being adjudicated for that crime, is a testament to the arbitrary nature of using racial identity as a criterion for prosecution in Indian country. Or, as was the case in *Oliphant*, the idea that someone could live in a community, assault a member of that community on community land, at an event hosted by that community, yet not be held accountable for their actions by that community, demonstrates the way that identity politics systematically strip Native peoples of their ability to exert meaningful control over the people and activities on their land.

Finally, since the Violence Against Women Reauthorization Act of 2013 (VAWA 2013), the type of assault, the relationship between the perpetrator and the survivor, and the relationship between the perpetrator and the Native community must also be defined in order to determine jurisdiction. While Title IX of VAWA 2013 challenges *Oliphant* to allow tribes to prosecute some non-Native perpetrators, it continues to complicate matters by using the nature of the perpetrator/victim and perpetrator/community relationship as determinants in jurisdiction (see Figures 3–5). Under VAWA 2013, tribes may exert some limited jurisdiction over non-Native offenders if: the perpetrator is an intimate, dating or spousal partner; or if the perpetrator has ties to Indian country as a resident, employee, or romantic partner of a Native community member. This most recent development in Indian country jurisdiction is theorized at length in Chapter Six, however the jurisdictional mechanics resulting from VAWA 2013 will be considered throughout this chapter.

Federal Declination and Impunity

Sexual assault cases in general are difficult to prosecute, but Indian country jurisdiction has exacerbated this challenge, leading to exceedingly high declination rates.[27] In Indian country, criminal proceedings often start with a "mini-trial" to determine jurisdiction.[28] From these mini-trials it could take weeks or months to determine whether jurisdiction is federal, state, tribal, or a combination of two or more sovereigns.[29] In the meantime, perpetrators can flee and evidence can be lost, mishandled, or degraded—all of which contribute to high declination rates.[30]

When criminal investigations focus on jurisdiction, evidence collection and interviewing people of interest are often postponed. And, if one sovereign entity does collect evidence, it may be thrown out by another agency that may have different standards for chain of custody, search warrants, and evidence collection. Until recently,[31] Indian Health Service (IHS) hospitals had no standard protocols for collecting sexual assault forensic information from Native women who had been raped, and often, this information was not collected at all. When evidence was collected, it was often mishandled or destroyed, and therefore inadmissible in court.[32]

Additionally, although the federal government has a responsibility for providing health care and other basic services to many Native communities, up until recently, IHS facilities often did not have sexual assault forensic examination kits. In some cases where Native women were raped in Indian country but taken to non-IHS hospitals, they were expected to pay for their own rape kits—which can cost between $700–$800.[33] This is a service that is usually provided free of charge for individuals who are part of a state investigation into sexual assault.

When evidence and investigation take a back seat to jurisdiction, it means that perpetrators are rarely arrested. In cases where a warrant is issued, often so much time has elapsed that perpetrators have fled.[34] In some cases, determining jurisdiction and collecting enough evidence for an arrest has caused law enforcement authorities to wait up to four years to arrest someone suspected of sexually assaulting a Native woman.[35]

As a result of Native advocacy around these disturbing trends, the federal government passed the Tribal Law and Order Act (TLOA) in 2010. This law was, among other things, designed to: increase intergovernmental communication by facilitating coordination between tribal, state and federal law enforcement bodies; prepare IHS facilities by developing uniform procedures and granting resources to manage sexual assault cases; and encourage accountability by tracking and publishing federal declination rates.[36]

The TLOA appears to have significantly lowered declination rates for sexual assault in Indian country.[37] However, while the TLOA signaled measured improvement in declination rates, they still remain disproportionately high. As Chapter Five will demonstrate, the TLOA legislated *over* the problem of jurisdictional conflicts without addressing the underlying issues that shape crime in Indian country. While the TLOA may have ameliorated some problems in the short term, it cannot dismantle the root problem in the long term, leaving us continuing to grapple with high rates of sexual assault against Native women.

Because of enduring problems with jurisdiction, often cases still do not result in arrests or referrals to state and/or federal governments. And even when jurisdiction can be determined, and enough evidence is collected for cases to be taken on by the federal government, attitudes and perceptions of Indian country also contribute to high declination rates. As former U.S. Attorney Margaret Chiara noted:

> I've had [assistant U.S. attorneys] look right at me and say, "I did not sign up for this" […] they want to do big drug cases, white-collar crime and conspiracy. And I'll tell you, the vast majority of judges feel the same way. They will look at these Indian country cases and say, "what is this doing here? I could have stayed in state court if I wanted this stuff." […] It's terrible indifference, which is dangerous because lives are involved.[38]

While the federal government colonized tribal jurisdiction under the rhetoric that Native people were incapable of managing serious crimes, today the United States often refuses to manage the duties it has appropriated. From a federal perspective, it appears that when crime in Indian country endangers white Americans sweeping legislation should be passed. However, when crime in Indian country affects Native women, it can be ignored in favor of what is seen as more important matters that primarily affect non-Native people. In other words, while crime in Indian country is too important to be left to Native people, it is not important enough to take resources away from white-collar crime. As federal prosecutors construct prosecuting sexual violence in Indian country as being inconsequential, they send the message that the lives and bodies of Native women are not valuable or worthy of protection. And, outside of the Native community itself, it appears that no one has heard this message louder than non-Native men.

Predatory Violence Against Native Women in the Wake of *Oliphant*

When traveling through Indian country, rather than falling under the jurisdiction of a sovereign by implied consent (such as when one crosses the border from one U.S. state to another, or travels from the U.S. to a foreign country), Indian country post-*Oliphant* is a space where the majority of non-Native people may enter a foreign sovereign, yet have no accountability to that sovereign. Jason O'Neal, the tribal police chief of the Chickasaw Nation, shows us what this reality looks like for tribal law enforcement in an interview with National Public Radio's Laura Sullivan. The interview takes place on Chickasaw land outside of a gas station convenience store:

Laura Sullivan:	Here's a guy walking into the store now. If he goes in there and he steals a carton of cigarettes, what happens to him?
Jason O'Neal:	If he's an Indian, he would go to jail.
LS:	If he is a non-Indian, what happens to him?
JO:	We would simply let him go and forward a report to the U.S. attorney.
LS:	And what happens to those reports?
JO:	Well, I really couldn't tell ya. I don't think I've ever been called back on one of them.[39]

Despite the fact that members of the federal government have recognized that "tribal justice systems are ultimately the most appropriate institutions for maintaining order in tribal communities,"[40] both state and federal governments continue to play competing roles in Indian country jurisdiction, creating a space in which law enforcement officers like O'Neal may be powerless to adjudicate crime committed by non-Native perpetrators. As one Native woman noted, because of this non-Native sexual predators have "targeted Indian country, reservations, rancherias and communities as the very best place to prey on Native women."[41]

In general, rape is an overwhelmingly intra-racial crime. For example, approximately 90% of Black women report being assaulted by a Black assailant and at least 70% of White women report being assaulted by a White assailant.[42] However, the Native community is the one glaring exception. For Native women, 86% of sexual assault is perpetrated by non-Native men, and four out of five Native survivors of sexual assault describe their attacker(s) as white.[43] This striking anomaly in sexual assault statistics does not exist in a vacuum. Rather, these statistics are dramatically shaped by the colonial context of jurisdiction in Indian country.

While all sexual assault is by nature violent, it does operate in different contexts. As discussed in Chapter One, the complicated system of jurisdictional authority in Indian country not only specifically privileges non-Native identity, but it also specifically marginalizes Native identity in cases of sexual violence. While jurisdiction over the sexual assault of *non*-Native women in Indian country defaults to the state, the involvement of a *Native* victim signals the interest of three separate sovereigns who may compete for jurisdiction—compromising the investigation of each—or decline to investigate, denying the Native survivor recourse for her assault.

As a result of the jurisdictional conflicts created by federal Indian policy, non-Native (overwhelmingly white) men become aware that their racial identity signals legal impunity, and in turn specifically seek out *Native* (as opposed to non-Native) women in *Indian country* as opposed to state land. One article in the *Native American Times* described sexual predators as viewing Indian country as "feeding grounds,"[44] where white men "can do whatever they want."[45] Another blog states "if you want to rape [...] somebody and get away with it, do it on an Indian reservation."[46] Others have described Indian country as a "free-for-all,"[47] where "rapists are allowed to roam reservations, attacking women and young girls without real fear of being punished."[48] And as Deborah Blossom (Western Shoshone), acting director of the Great Basin Women's Coalition Against Violence stated, "Our women are open game. So many are violated and they tell us no one will do anything."[49]

The ease with which non-Native men may sexually violate Native women sends the message that the bodily integrity of Native women is not to be respected, that crime against Native women simply does not matter, and that Native women by their very racial and gender identities are inherently rapable. Viewing sexual violence through this predatory lens reveals that the disturbing rates of sexual assault against Native women today are in fact only contemporary manifestations of a colonial legacy hundreds of years in the making.

The Colonial Context of Sexual Violence: Constructing the Native "Other"

Sexual violence against Native women, while virtually unheard of prior to European contact, became an immediate reality in the first interactions between American Indians and Europeans.[50] Journal entries by early colonizers and letters from early settlers in the Americas detailed the ways that Native women were singled out for systematic rape.[51] Often, these assaults were characterized as collateral damage—that in the primary project of seizing Native land, European colonizers were also able to seize Native women. However, a more nuanced examination reveals that sexual violence against Native women was—and continues to be—central to the colonial experience.

As noted in Chapter Three, when Europeans first arrived in the Americas they confronted lands and resources that they were eager to make their own. At the same time, they also confronted Native peoples with distinct social, political and legal rights to these resources. Legal justifications thus quickly lent themselves as tools to legitimate the theft of the land and resources desired by European colonizers. However, just because something is legal, doesn't mean that it's moral.[52] For example, if murder were legal, most of us still wouldn't kill others because we recognize that other people share our humanity. Therefore appropriating Native land at the expense of Native people had to be naturalized through more than just law. It is in this context that ideological constructions of Native people emerged as a corollary to moralize European conquest itself.[53] By portraying Native people as savage, barbaric, and sub-human, European colonizers were able to justify their legal actions.[54] As author Thomas Jimson notes:

> When you set about to dispossess a people of their land and source of livelihood, unless you have no conscious at all, one must find an excuse to safely hide from the truth of pain and suffering you are inflicting on innocent peoples […] If, indeed, [Indians] were human beings […] then they were in fact a lesser type of humanity who had no rights to life, land, or liberty.[55]

Jimson's passage demonstrates how ideology structured the legalization of what would otherwise be considered theft and murder. And, while these notions were levied against entire Native nations, they were highly gendered as narratives of conquest often focused on the perceptions of Native women.

At the same time that Europeans confronted Native communities with pre-existing rights to lands and resources, they also encountered Native women who were central political actors in the nations that governed these resources. And because many Native communities were matrilineal, women were often the ones who controlled and regulated the lands and resources that colonizers wanted.[56] Here, women's political and economic power threatened the primary goals of European colonization. Therefore, as Native activist Brenda Hill (Siksika Blackfeet) notes, "Attempts to destroy tribal sovereignty began with the destruction of women's sovereignty."[57]

As colonizers realized that divesting entire communities of their resources necessitated the disenfranchisement of Native women in particular, constructing the Native woman as a dangerous "Other" was a crucial tool of conquest. As political equals in their communities, Native women not only played central roles in civic life, but also made affirmative decisions about their bodies, gender expression, and sexuality. In contrast, Western Euro-patriarchy excluded women from the public sphere, and policed the bodies and sexuality of women.[58] As a result, European encounters with women who were not dominated by men became the foundation on which the subhuman status of Native women (and by extension entire Native communities) was built. In this context, European constructions of Native communities as savage were both gendered and sexualized, as many contact-era accounts indicate. For example in a 1525 letter to the Council of the Indies, Dominican Friar Tomas Ortiz remarked of Native people:

> They are more given to sodomy than any other nation. There is no justice among them. They go naked. They have no respect either for love or for virginity. They are stupid and silly. They have no respect for truth, save when it is to their advantage.

> They are unstable. They have no knowledge of what foresight means [...] They are incapable of learning.[59]

In this passage, Native communities were classified as having no justice, as unintelligent, and as sexually immoral. Such ideological constructions lent themselves to colonists eager to justify the appropriation of Native resources. If Native people had no justice, the logic went, they were by nature dangerous and violence against them became an act of self-defense. If they were unintelligent, then they were not able to manage their own resources, thus naturalizing European appropriation. If their bodies were not dominated by Christian morals, then they were available for domination by Western Europeans, which normalized gender violence against Native women. And indeed, from first contact, this mindset justified sexual violence against Native women, enslavement, and the appropriation of Native lands and natural resources.[60]

While Native people in general were seen as dangerous and sexually perverse, Native women were particularly vilified. Not only did Native women present a moral danger through perceived sexual perversion, but also their sexuality was presented as a physical danger to men. This is documented throughout the writings of Amerigo Vespucci, an Italian explorer, cartographer, and namesake of the Americas. From 1497 to 1504, Vespucci wrote a series of journal entries and letters regarding his alleged[61] voyages to the so-called New World. In one letter he described the unbridled lust of Native women as being so powerful that it led to the sterilization of men. Vespucci wrote, "[Native] women, being very libidinous" would engorge men's genitals to the point that they would "lose their virile organs and remain eunuchs."[62] Vespucci went on to illustrate that Native women's innate savagery and insatiable hunger for men drove them to literally consume European men. In a letter from his alleged third voyage, Vespucci recounted:

> [We] saw a [Native] woman come from the hill, carrying a great stick in her hand. When she came to where our Christian stood, she raised it, and gave him such a blow that he was felled to the ground. The other [Native] women immediately took him by the feet, and dragged him towards the hill [...] they all ran away towards the hill, where the women were still tearing the Christian to pieces. At a great fire they had made they roasted him before our eyes, showing us many pieces, and then eating them.[63]

Vespucci's piece communicates the savagery of Native communities as a whole through the cannibalistic appetite of Native women for European men. This narrative of consumption was highly sexualized throughout Vespucci's writings. In the same piece, he went on to portray Native women's desires as not only leading to literal emasculation and consumption, but ultimately to the moral corruption of "Christian" (European) men:

> [Native men] marry as many wives as they please; and son cohabits with mother, brother with sister, male cousin with female, and any man with the first woman he meets.[64] [...] The women as I have said go about naked and are very libidinous, yet their bodies are comely; but they are as wild as can be imagined.[65] [...] When [Native women] had the opportunity of copulating with Christians, urged by excessive lust, they defiled and prostituted themselves.[66]

Vespucci's description of the perversion of Native people generally, is structured by the danger of Native women's sexuality specifically. The choice of Native women to "defile" and "prostitute" themselves, when framed through its impact on European men, shows that Native women not only posed a threat to men's physical bodies, but also to their Christian morals. In Vespucci's eyes, as Native women lusted after Christians, it threatened the morality of European men who may succumb to Native women's unrelenting sexual urges. And because Europeans perceived Native women as choosing to *embrace* this savage sexuality, they then became constructed as having no bodily integrity at all.

As Cherokee anti-violence activist Andrea Smith points out, prostitutes are rarely believed when they report that they have been raped.[67] This is because prostitutes are constructed as always inviting sex and therefore maintain no bodily integrity. Similarly, this construction of Native women as having no sexual mores appeared to invite sexual assault and naturalize rape by European colonizers. As Michele de Cuneo, an Italian nobleman on Columbus's second voyage wrote:

> While I was in the boat, I captured a very beautiful Carib woman, whom said Lord Admiral gave to me, and with whom, having taken her into my cabin, she being naked according to their custom, I conceived desire to take pleasure. I wanted to put my desire into execution but she did not want it and treated me with her finger nails in such a manner that I wished I had never begun. But seeing that, (to tell you the end of it all), I took a rope and thrashed her well, for which she raised such unheard of screams that you would not have believed your ears. Finally we came to an agreement in such manner that I can tell you she seemed to have been brought up in a school of harlots.[68]

In this passage, the very identity of this woman as Native played an active role in her rape. As a Native "Other" she was objectified and able to be "given" to the perpetrator. As it was her "custom" to be naked, and it was this nakedness that invited her rape, her very identity as a Native woman naturalized her sexual assault. Because she did not fit European gender roles and cultural norms, the woman in this passage was constructed as having no bodily integrity and therefore her assault became justified in the eyes of her rapist. In fact, the author felt so vindicated by his actions he was able to conclude that despite her initial resistance, she ultimately enjoyed her violent assault.

Of course "enjoying rape" is a contradiction in terms, but the audacity of the author to frame his assault as such illustrates the extreme nature of colonial attitudes towards Native women. If Native women are seen as a threat to men, then violence against them becomes an act of self-defense. If Native women are constructed as lascivious, then all sexual activity is invited and ultimately enjoyed. And finally, if Native women appear to choose to live in bodies that are not yet subdued by patriarchy, then they are available to be dominated by European men.

Despite the notion of Native women "defiling" and "prostituting" themselves to European men while ultimately enjoying sexual assault, the reality is that Native women actively resisted rape. This was illustrated in the previous passage and is supported by many additional narratives. For example in 1552's *The Devastation of the Indies: A Brief Account,* Dominican Friar and Spanish historian Bartolomé De Las Casas recounted both the violence committed against Native women as well as the extent to which they were willing to resist it:

> One Spaniard took a maiden by force to commit the sin of the flesh with her, dragging her away from her mother, finally having to unsheathe his sword to cut off the woman's hands and when the damsel still resisted they stabbed her to death.[69]

This example, while tragic, shows the extent to which Native women resisted sexual violence.[70] And like the previous example, De Las Casas's account challenges the notion that Native women enjoyed or passively accepted sexual assault.

Over 200 years later, Franciscan Friar Junípero Serra recorded similar accounts as he presided over the missionary conquest of what would become the American state of California. During his tenure, he noted the rampant sexual assault of Native women by Spanish soldiers and attempted to intervene by documenting the attacks. One such document from 1773 reads:

> When both men and women at the sight of [Spanish soldiers] would take off running [...] the soldiers, adept as they are at lassoing cows and mules, would lasso Indian women who then became prey for their unbridled lust.[71]

Serra's advocacy ultimately made little difference in the lives of Native women who were terrorized by Spanish soldiers, as his dependence on them to police California Indian people outweighed his desire to end sexual violence.[72] Despite Serra's ineffective campaign, his 1773 letter reveals a spirit of resistance as Native women actively engaged agency to avoid sexual assault.

Antonia Castañeda "Sexual Violence in the Politics and Policies of Conquest: Amerindian Women and the Spanish Conquest of Alta California" documents this and other forms of resistance throughout California's mission history in which Native women evaded sexual assault by fleeing, hiding, and campaigning against the missionary system in its entirety. For example, in 1785 a young Tongva spiritual leader named Toypurina was able to unite six disparate Native communities and organize an armed rebellion against the San Gabriel Mission. The rebellion centered on Native oppression under the missions as a whole, but was particularly inspired by the gendered persecution of Toypurina herself whose power as a cultural and political leader was seen as particularly threatening by Spanish colonizers.[73]

These passages not only show the prevalence of sexual assault during the early eras of colonization, but also the force with which Native women exerted agency against it. Yet, despite this clear tradition of resistance, colonial constructions of Native women continued to portray them as licentious and therefore lacking bodily integrity. As this next section will show, these initial perceptions of Native women have continued to impact their corporal sovereignty, as the trajectory of American colonial expansion continues to be structured by sexual violence.

Figure 7. Indian Female of the Arrowauka Nation.

John Gabriel Stedman, *Narrative of a Five Years' Expedition*—1796

The Taíno of the Arawak Nation were among the first Indigenous people to encounter Columbus. John Gabriel Stedman's written accounts of Arawak women include numerous references to nudity and to a perceived lack of bodily shame. Michele de Cuneo's journal entry from Columbus's second voyage (discussed earlier in this chapter) demonstrates how these perceptions of Native women justified sexual assault in the eyes of European men. Courtesy of the California State Library- Sutro Branch, San Francisco, California.

Figure 8. Engraving from Part Five.
Livinus Hulsius, *Collection of Voyages and Travels*—1599

(*Above*) This illustration from Livinus Hulsius' *Collection of Voyages and Travels* accompanies Sir Walter Raleigh's sixteenth-century account of the so-called New World. Here, a nude Native woman stands casually in the foreground. In the background, nude men and women are coupled in various stages of intimate encounters. The scene reflects European notions of Indigenous Americans as untamed and hypersexual. The perception that Native women willingly displayed their bodies, engaged in casual sexual relationships, and thus lacked sexual mores, contributed to the European assumption that they could then make no claims to bodily integrity. Courtesy of the John Carter Brown Library at Brown University.

(*Opposite*) *In The Four Continents* a bare-breasted, armed Native woman personifies America for a European audience. In her left arm she holds a human leg, severed at the thigh and ankle. In the background, Native people butcher a man and roast his leg on a spit—a common theme in contact era imagery used to communicate savagery and danger. A poem accompanying the image conveys America as a land of extraordinary wealth that is inhabited by a people of "barbarous rudenes [sic]." The author positions Christianity as a source of intervention where God's "Grace" will dress the nude barbarian and where the "Sunshine of Godds love [sic]" will cast out the "gloomy Shades of Death [sic]." © The Trustees of the British Museum.

Figure 9. America.
John Stafford, *The Four Continents*—1625–1635

Figure 10. America.

Adriaen Collaert after Maerten de Vos, *The Four Continents*—1588–89

(*Above*) Adriaen Collaert's sixteenth-century representation of America depicts an armed Native woman seated on an armadillo as a battle between Indigenous people and Europeans rages in the background. Behind her are Native people butchering a man and roasting his leg on a spit. The Latin inscription below the image refers to a land rich with gold but inhabited by a dangerous people. The Metropolitan Museum of Art, Gift of the Estate of James Hazen Hyde, 1959 www.metmuseum.org

(*Opposite*) Volume XI of *Atlas Maior* includes some of the earliest and most complete maps of the Americas. Opening the volume is this illustration of an armed Native woman standing on the decapitated, arrow-pierced head of a European man. In the background, Native men toil in a silver mine and present the precious metal at her feet. To Europeans, America represented both the promise of riches and the danger of Native women who controlled them. *Volume XI: America*, Tracy W. McGregor Library of American History, Albert and Shirley Small Special Collections Library, University of Virginia.

Figure 11. America.
Joan Blaeu, *Atlas Maior*—1665

Figure 12. Discovery of America: Vespucci Landing in America.
Jan van der Straet (called Stradanus)—1587–89

(*Above*) Figure twelve depicts Amerigo Vespucci's so-called discovery[74] of America. The word "ACIREMA" in backwards letters bridges the Atlantic Ocean to what would become the United States. Here, Vespucci confronts a Native woman who represents both the promise and the danger of the New World. Though relaxing on a hammock, she has a club nearby and is surrounded by wild animals. In the distance, Native people roast a human leg on a spit. The Metropolitan Museum of Art, Gift of the Estate of James Hazen Hyde, 1959 www.metmuseum.org

(*Opposite*) Part Eleven of Theodor de Bry's *Indiae Orientalis* compiles Amerigo Vespucci's letters from his 1501 and 1503 voyages to America. The engraving illustrates a scene discussed earlier in this chapter in which Vespucci recalls Native women capturing European men, butchering their bodies, and publically consuming their flesh. Though the background of the image clearly portrays conflict between Native people and Europeans as a whole, the violence perpetrated by Native women against European men is at the forefront of Vespucci's narrative and de Bry's corresponding illustration. Courtesy of the John Carter Brown Library at Brown University.

PARS UNDECIMA ORIENTALIS.

I.

Quid Americo Vesputio, ejúsque comitibus, in India orientali inter Barbaros evenerit.

AMericus Vesputius ad quandam Indiæ Orientalis insulam delatus, omni ope familiaritatem cum nudis incolis contrahere conatus est: cùm verò planè agrestes, nulla ratione ad humaniorem mentem inflecti possent, naves rursum conscendit, relictis in littore nolis, speculis, aliisq; id genus crepundiis, ad quæ contemplanda statim mulierum barbararum confluxit agmen. Interea Vesputius venusta facie adolescentem, qui isti mulierum turbæ sese immisceret, ablegat. Hunc fœminæ undique prensantes, habitum ejus non parùm miratæ, circumsistunt. Tandem una à tergo accedens fustem tanta vi capiti Adolescentis impingit, ut mortuus in terram corrueret: statim reliquæ eum in collem vicinum protrahunt, vestibus exutum mactant, torrent, atque in Lusitanorum conspectu vorant. Viri verò magno impetu Lusitanos invadunt, qui metu exterriti; armorum planè immemores, fugam capessunt, cúmque minori scaphâ, quæ sabulo adhæserat, tam subitò ad majorem navem se recipere non possent, non parùm à Barbaris istis damni acceperunt: donec periculo in majoribus navibus cognito, quatuor tormenta, absque ullo tamen damno, in Barbaros evibrarent; quorum fragore & crepitu attoniti in fugam sese conjecerunt.

a 2 Quomo-

Figure 13. Engraving from Part Eleven.
Theodor de Bry, *Indiae Orientalis*—1619

The Colonial Context of Sexual Violence: Gendering the Body, Gendering the Land

The social construction of Native women as sexually promiscuous and therefore sexually violable helps to contextualize the widespread rape of Native women within the larger project of colonization. As Europeans and later Euro-Americans conceptualized the "New World," it was envisioned in very gendered and sexualized terms. Through colonists' eyes, Native land was "virgin," "bountiful," "unbridled," "untamed," and "free for the taking."[75] Not coincidentally, the Indigenous female bodies on this land were imbued with the same sexualized discourse. Here, under Euro-American colonization, the construction of Native women as having no *corporal* sovereignty over their own bodies became fused with attitudes towards Native people as having no *political* sovereignty over their own land.

In Kirkpatrick Sale's *Conquest of Paradise: Christopher Columbus and the Columbian Legacy,* the author demonstrates the ways that the colonization of the Americas was seen largely in gendered terms as perceptions of Native land went hand-in-hand with perceptions of Native women's bodies. Sale notes that America became "the succulent maiden to be seduced, deflowered, and plundered by a virile Europe [...]"[76] Here, the technological prowess of Europe was substituted for male sexual prowess as the rape of Indian land became the rape of Indian women. Sale goes on to argue:

> [T]he masculine attitude toward the feminine, the acquisitive toward the desired, the dominant toward the weak, the civilized toward the natural: the women of America were as much a part of the bounty due the conquering Europeans as the other resources in which it luxuriated [...] attitudes toward sex and women [were] every bit as exploitative and instrumental as those toward nature: Mother Earth and earth mother were all one, and all to be used.[77]

As the author indicates, conflating Native land with Native sexuality was central to colonization, as the conquest of Native land was structured by the conquest of Native women.[78] As bodies became objects analogous to what was to be consumed, Native land—like Native women—became something to be conquered, domesticated and subdued by Euro-American men.

After the formation of the United States, European attitudes towards land became increasingly entrenched in federal Indian law. Perhaps the most significant example of this is the 1823 U.S. Supreme Court decision in *Johnson v. M'Intosh* where the court ruled that private citizens could not purchase land directly from Native people.[79] Chief Justice John Marshall who delivered the majority opinion in the case supported the ruling by arguing that Native nations did not have complete legal authority over their own land because they had failed to privatize it.[80] After *Johnson*, Native people were henceforth considered merely "occupants" of lands that they wandered over but never actually owned.[81] By contrast, through the capacity to dominate the earth through extraction and privatization, Europeans (and later Euro-Americans who inherited the land after American independence) became the rightful "owners" of American land.

Under *Johnson*, Native people's rights to their land were minimized because of their failure to dominate it. Similarly, the logic of sexual violence is itself structured from these European perceptions of land and political sovereignty. Under Euro-American colonization, Native women were seen as having no bodily integrity and a savage sexuality that appeared to invite rape. As bodies were constructed as analogous to land that had yet to be dominated and was therefore for the taking, Native women were constructed as simply occupants of a body that was destined to be dominated by European power.[82] Because Native sexuality, like Native land, was "free" and "unbridled," it was not for Native women to control. Instead Native women's bodies became something that should be subdued at the hands of Euro-American men. Like land, ownership of Native bodies could only come from patriarchal domination and the inscription of violence.[83]

While the conflation of land and bodies may appear to portray sexual violence against Native women merely as an aspect of colonization, Native scholar Andrea Smith illustrates that instead it is central to it.[84] In *Conquest*, Smith cites Paula Gunn Allen to argue:

> [C]olonizers realized that in order to subjugate indigenous nations they would have to subjugate women within these nations. Native peoples needed to learn the value of hierarchy, the role of physical abuse in maintaining that hierarchy, and the importance of women remaining submissive to their men.[85]

Smith goes on to note, "Thus in order to colonize a people whose society was not hierarchical, colonizers must first naturalize hierarchy through instituting patriarchy."[86]

As Smith and Allen argue, in order for Euro-Americans to successfully colonize Native resources, they had to successfully subjugate Native women. Sexual violence against Native women thus became a tool with which to inscribe hierarchies on non-hierarchical peoples in order to control communities as a whole.

Sale, Smith, and Allen's analyses indicate the way that the early conflation of Native sexuality, Native bodies, and Native resources informed the colonial process. As Euro-American hegemony expanded, it continued to signal widespread sexual violence against Native women as rape became incorporated into colonial law and policy. Spanish Dominican Bartolomé De Las Casas, for example, described how the wives of male Native leaders were strategically raped as a method to control entire Native communities.[87] Later, the Doolittle Report of 1867 issued by the U.S. federal government detailed the ways in which sexual violence against Native women was integrated as a weapon of war in the military conquest of Native peoples.[88]

Violence against Native women was in fact so extreme that Native women were not just sexually assaulted, but murdered and then mutilated. The federal government's own reports reveal that after the Camp Grant massacre of 1871, Native women were found "lying in such a position, and from the appearance of their genital organs and of their wounds, there can be no doubt that they were first ravished and then shot dead."[89] And after the Sand Creek Massacre of 1864, Lieutenant James Connor remarked that he "heard of numerous instances in which men had cut out the private parts of [slain Native women] and stretched them over their saddle-bows and wore them over their hats while riding in the ranks."[90]

As these examples show, Native women were not only raped and murdered, but their sexual organs literally became objects that were appropriated by white men as symbols of conquest. And as the federal government waged war against American Indians in westward expansion, large-scale violence against Native women became incorporated as an active strategy. For example, prior to ascending to the presidency, then General Andrew Jackson waged war against Native nations in the American South to free up land for the Southern plantation economy. As part of his military strategy, he is said to have instructed his troops to specifically kill women and children to "complete" the "extermination."[91] Similarly, as Colonel John Chivington prepared to invade Cheyenne and Arapaho land to protect the interests of white settlers during the Indian Wars, he advised his troops to specifically kill Native women and children because "nits make lice."[92]

Both Jackson and Chivington's statements illustrate the gendered aspects of colonization that identify Native women as the ultimate threat to the settler-state. As the colonization of the Americas has primarily been about the appropriation of Native resources and the expansion of Euro-American cultural hegemony, those who have stood in the way of this project were considered problematic and polluting to the body politic.[93] As the bearers of future generations who would continue to make claims over the economic resources of the Americas, Native women's fertility posed a constant threat.[94] Therefore solving the "Indian problem" necessitated targeting Native women and their ability to reproduce.[95]

In *Conquest*, Andrea Smith illustrates that reproductive violence against Native women is still part and parcel to federal Indian policy today. Her work shows the way that Native women's fertility has been targeted through environmental racism, forced/coerced sterilization and adoption, and medical testing of dangerous drugs.

Here, Smith shows how Indian Health Service policies sanctioned the widespread surgical sterilization of Native women without informed consent and also limited Native women's fertility by experimenting with dangerous contraceptives like Norplant and Depo-Provera.[96] Smith's research confirms my personal experience as a Case Worker for the Washoe Tribe in which I encountered clients who had been forced or coerced into medical procedures that rendered them sterile, as well as with my experience at Sacred Circle's *Women are Sacred* conference, in which Native women shared their stories of forced adoption. Andrea Smith also builds on existing environmental racism research to note that the colonization of Native land with toxic debris simultaneously colonizes Native women's bodies and reproductive organs.[97] As Smith and others show, when radioactive waste sterilizes Native women and/or causes debilitating birth defects and stillborn babies, the colonization of the land *is literally* the colonization of Native women's bodies.

Conclusion: Jurisdiction as Sexual Violence

As a settler-state, the United States—by definition—can only exist through the consumption of Native lands and resources. As such, the existence of Native people with rights to those lands and resources is an existential threat. As this chapter shows, "solving" the "problem" of Native political autonomy directed colonial violence towards Native women in particular. Here, the nation-state has attempted to disempower entire communities *politically* by attacking women *corporally*.

Nez Perce/Tejana scholar Inés Hernández-Avila tells us, "It is *because* of a Native American woman's sex that she is hunted down and slaughtered, in fact, singled out because she has the potential through childbirth to insure the continuance of the people"[98] (emphasis in original). Through their ability to reproduce, Native women may usher into the world successive generations of Native people who will continue to threaten the legitimacy of the settler-state. As such, the nation-state has consistently hunted down Native women to be demoralized, dismembered and disappeared.

Today, Native women continue to be singled out and, in fact, hunted down by non-Native men in the colonial space that is Indian country.[99] Today when white men target Native women for sexual violence in Indian country, this is both an individual action of sexual violence, as well as a larger, societal act of colonial violence. As individual men learn of their privileged racial statuses and use this privilege to specifically target and inscribe sexual violence on Native women, it becomes impossible to separate the individual predator from the predatory society that has preyed upon Native women since contact.

Euro-American colonization was made possible through legal violence that codified Native people as barbaric and incapable of maintaining control over their own lands and resources. As part of this process, in an attempt to "solve" the "Indian problem," federal Indian policy created modern jurisdictional conflicts. The Major Crimes Act, the Dawes Act, Public Law 280, and *Oliphant v. Suquamish Indian Tribe* are all acts of legal violence marked by investments in American hegemony and legitimated through the construction of Native people as savage and backwards. Similarly, the creation of Indian country and the establishment of a nation-state that may create such policies could not have occurred without violence against Native women. "Indian country" itself was forged from legal violence and warfare, both of which were structured by the logic of sexual violence as a tool to disempower entire communities. And it is in these spaces—created from the construction of Native women as savage and therefore rapable—in which they are again violated with impunity. Therefore, when a white man targets Native women for sexual violence in these spaces, he does so with the force of 500 years of colonial history.

In this way, we must see jurisdictional impunity in the prosecution of sexual violence against Native women not simply as the unintended consequence of a complex but necessary legal structure, but instead as a colonial phenomenon that actively *maintains* and *inscribes* colonial violence on the bodies of Native women. As such, addressing American jurisdiction and the sexual violence that characterizes it requires us to call Euro-American colonization itself into question. As jurisdictional conflicts and sexual violence continue to plague Indian country, Native women, Native communities, non-Native organizations and the U.S. federal government are crafting solutions. Based on our understanding of the way that sexual, legal, and colonial violence operate within jurisdictional schema in Indian country, the remainder of this book turns its attention to evaluating solutions in an attempt to contribute to the anti-violence movement in Indian country.

Notes

1. Andy Ternay, "How to Rape a Woman and Get Away With It." *Native American Net Roots*. Web. 21 Jul. 2008 <www.nativeamerican netroots.net/diary/130/> Accessed 12 Apr. 2011.
2. Deer, "Sovereignty of the Soul" 458.
3. Ibid.
4. Pevar, *Rights of Indians and Tribes* 119. There are some exceptions to this which are discussed in Figures 1–6 and their footnotes.
5. Meisner, "Modern Problems."
6. Major Crimes Act 18 U.S.C. § 1153 (1885).
7. Pevar, *The Rights of Indians and Tribes* 149.

8. Deer and Garrow, *Tribal Criminal Law* 87–93.
9. Perry, *Policing Race* 42–45.
10. Ibid., 43.
11. Ibid.
12. Ibid., 42–45.
13. Sullivan,"Legal Hurdles Stall Rape Cases."
14. Interview with an assistant U.S. attorney (identity withheld), quoted from Amnesty International, *Maze* 34. This is substantiated by reports from the *Native American Times* stating "In Oklahoma it can take weeks or even months to determine jurisdiction." ("US Authorities Fail to Protect Native American and Alaska Native Women from Shocking Rates of Rape, Reports Amnesty International," *Native American Times* 27 Apr. 2007: 1–2).
15. Interview with support worker May 2005. As quoted in Amnesty International, *Maze* 27.
16. Deer and Garrow, *Tribal Criminal Law* 87–93.
17. Ibid.
18. Hallie Bongar White et al., "2008 Final Report: Creative Civil Remedies Against Non-Indian Offenders in Indian Country," *Southwest Center for Law and Policy* (Tucson: 2008) 14.
19. Pevar, *The Rights of Indians and Tribes* 18.
20. Hallie Bongar White et al., "Final Report" 7.
21. All charts generated from data in Garrow and Deer's *Tribal Criminal Law and Procedure,* 93–94 and S. 47: Violence Against Women Reauthorization Act of 2013.
22. See Figure 6 for exceptions. U.S. military jurisdiction may also act as a fourth sovereign (as in the case of *Elk v. U.S.*).
23. There are some exceptions to this when the federal government shares jurisdiction with the state for certain crimes (e.g., hate crimes committed exclusively on state land that also violate federal civil rights laws). In that case, the state and the federal government would have concurrent jurisdiction as separate sovereigns and double jeopardy would not attach. As noted in Figure 1, U.S. military jurisdiction may also play a role for certain crimes.
24. Lujan and Adams, "US Colonization of Indian Justice" 12.
25. Ibid.
26. White et al., "Final Report" 8.
27. For example: between 1997 and 2006, the declination rate for federal crimes originating in Indian country was twice the rate of federally prosecuted crime in general; and in 2006, of the approximately 5,900 aggravated assaults referred to federal prosecutors only about 4% were prosecuted. See: Michael Riley, "Promises, Justice Broken: A Dysfunctional System Lets Serious Reservation Crimes Go Unpunished and Puts Indians at Risk," *Denver Post.* 11 Nov. 2007.
28. Amnesty International, *Maze* 62.
29. Ibid., 63.
30. Ibid., 27–28.
31. The passage of the Tribal Law and Order Act of 2010 implements sexual assault protocols in Indian Health Service hospitals. Pub L. No 111-211.
32. Amnesty International, *Maze* 58–59.

33. Amnesty International, *Maze.*
34. Ibid.
35. As Navajo Police Chief Jim Benally stated: "In the Navajo Nation, because violent crimes are investigated by FBI and prosecuted by US attorneys it can take up to 2–4 years for an arrest to be made." From Amnesty International *Maze of Injustice: The Failure to Protect Indigenous Women From Sexual Violence in the USA: One Year Update* (New York: Amnesty International Publications, 2008) 6.
36. Tribal Law and Order Act. Pub L. No 111-211. 29 Jul. 2010.
37. For example, recent Department of Justice reports show that declination rates for Indian country criminal cases rates have declined from about 50% to between 31% and 36% in the years since the signing of the TLOA. See United States Department of Justice, "Indian Country Investigations and Prosecutions." 2011–2012 and 2013.
38. Riley, "Promises, Justice Broken."
39. Sullivan, "Legal Hurdles Stall Rape Cases."
40. Janet Reno, "A Federal Commitment to Tribal Justice Systems," (79 Judicature 1995) 113–114.
41. Gray, "Protecting Indian Women" 8.
42. See USDOJ statistics as quoted in Amnesty International, *Maze* 4–5; and Steven Perry, "Measuring Crime and Justice in Indian Country," *Bureau of Justice Statistics*: 9–10, 18.
43. Ibid.
44. Gray, "Protecting Indian Women."
45. Quoting Chickasaw Tribal Police Chief Jason O'Neal in Sullivan, "Legal Hurdles Stall Rape Cases."
46. Wetzelbill, "I Was Witness to One on My Reservation," Comment on One in Three Native American Women Will Be Raped in Her Lifetime, 2007.
47. Sullivan, "Lawmakers Move to Curb Rape."
48. Chuck Cook, "Rape with Impunity: Police Shrug at 'Non-Emergency' Crime," *Indian Country Today* 70.20 (1987): 7.
49. Norrell, "Native Women Are Prey."
50. Mihesuah, *Indigenous American Women.*
51. See for example Bartolomé De Las Casas, *The Devastation of the Indies: A Brief Account* (Baltimore: The Johns Hopkins University Press) 1992. Originally published in 1542; and letters from Columbus's first and second voyages (1492–1496) published in John Cohen, *The Four Voyages of Christopher Columbus* (New York: Penguin, 1969).
52. As Martin Luther King Jr. reminded us in his letter from Birmingham jail as he sat incarcerated for protesting against civil rights violations of Black Americans, "We should never forget that everything Adolf Hitler did in Germany was 'legal.'" See Jonathan Rieder, *Gospel of Freedom: Martin Luther King Jr.'s Letter from Birmingham Jail and the Struggle that Changed a Nation* (New York: Bloomsbury Press, 2013) 68.
53. Mihesuah, *Indigenous American Women* 58–59.
54. Agtuca, "Beloved Women" 8.
55. Thomas Jimson, *Reflections on Manifest Destiny and Race.* Center for World Indigenous Studies, 1992.
56. Smith, *Conquest* 18.

57. Hill, "The Role of Advocates" 194.
58. See Mihesuah, "Colonialism and Disempowerment" in *Indigenous American Women.*
59. As quoted in Stannard, *American Holocaust* 217.
60. See generally, Howard Zinn *The People's History of the United States* (New York: HarperCollins, 2003); Smith, *Conquest*; and Kirkpatrick Sale, *Christopher Columbus and The Conquest of Paradise* (New York: Alfred Knopf, 1990).
61. In the introduction to *The Letters of Amerigo Vespucci,* translator Clements R. Markham discusses whether or not Vespucci actually made the journeys that he describes in his written accounts. Markham notes that many scholars (both contemporaries of Vespucci as well as modern historians) agree that some of Vespucci's letters were fabricated. For the purposes of this research, the veracity of Vespucci's accounts is somewhat moot. While his actual experiences may be questioned, there is no doubt that Vespucci's writing did significantly impact European/Euro-American attitudes towards the so-called New World. Since my discussion focuses on European/Euro-American *perceptions* of Native people, Vespucci's writing (fabricated or not) is therefore relevant. See Clements R. Markham trans. *The Letters of Amerigo Vespucci and Other Documents Illustrative of His Career* (New York: Burt Franklin, 2011).
62. Amerigo Vespucci, "Letter on his Third Voyage from Amerigo Vespucci to Lorenzo Pietro Francesco Di Medici" March (or April) 1503. From Markham *The Letters of Amerigo Vespucci.*
63. Vespucci, "Third Voyage of Amerigo Vespucci." From Markham *The Letters of Amerigo Vespucci.*
64. Vespucci as quoted in Kirkpatrick Sale, *Christopher Columbus and the Conquest of Paradise* (New York: Alfred Knopf, 1990) 141.
65. Vespucci, "Third Voyage of Amerigo Vespucci." From Markham *The Letters of Amerigo Vespucci* (alternative translation from Sale).
66. Vespucci as quoted in Sale, *Conquest of Paradise* 141.
67. Smith, *Conquest* 10.
68. As quoted in Stannard, *American Holocaust* 84.
69. De Las Casas, *Devastation* 77.
70. It is important to note that resistance to sexual assault can take many forms. Resistance does not have to involve a physical fight, or resisting to the point of death in order to be legitimate. All forms of resistance are important and valid.
71. Notes written by Junipero Serra circa 1773. Quoted in Antonia Castañeda, "Sexual Violence in the Politics and Policies of Conquest: Amerindian Women and the Spanish Conquest of Alta California," *Building With Our Hands: New Directions in Chicana Studies*, eds. Adela De La Torre and Beatriz M. Pesquera (Berkeley: University of California Press, 1993) 15.
72. Antonia Castañeda, "Sexual Violence in the Politics and Policies of Conquest."
73. Louis V. Jeffredo-Warden, "Perceiving, Experiencing, and Expressing the Sacred: An Indigenous Southern Californian View," *Over the Edge: Remapping the American West*, eds. Valerie J. Matsumoto and Blake Allmendinger (London: University of California Press, 1999) 330.
74. Though Columbus is credited with making first European contact with the so-called New World, it is Vespucci who is alleged to have made first landfall on what would become the

United States. Vespucci's first name (Latin: Americus) is the namesake of America. Ironically, the account of Vespucci's first voyage pictured above is likely a fabrication.

75. Deer, "Sovereignty of the Soul" 459; C. Richard King, "De/Scribing Squ*w: Indigenous Women and Imperial Idioms in the United States," *American Indian Culture and Research Journal,* UCLA American Indian Studies Center. 27.2 (2003): 6; Sale, *Conquest of Paradise* 141, 258; Albert Hurtado, "When Strangers Met: Sex and Gender on Three Frontiers," *Frontiers* 17.2 (1996): 57–59.
76. Sale, *Conquest of Paradise* 258.
77. Ibid., 141.
78. Perry, *Policing Race and Place* 33–34.
79. *Johnson v. M'Intosh* was the first of three U.S. Supreme Court cases known as "The Marshall Trilogy," which laid the foundation for modern federal Indian policy.
80. Barker, "For Whom Sovereignty Matters" *Sovereignty Matters:* 7–9.
81. Ibid.
82. Francis Jennings, "Virgin Land and Savage People," *American Quarterly* 23.4 (1971): 520–521.
83. Ibid.
84. Andrea Smith, "Not an Indian Tradition: The Sexual Colonization of Native Peoples," *Hypatia* 18.2 (Spring 2003): 70.
85. Quoting Paula Gunn Allen in Smith, *Conquest* 23.
86. Ibid.
87. De Las Casas, *Devastation of the Indies* 37.
88. *Condition of the Indian Tribes*. Report of the Joint Special Committee (Washington, D.C.: Government Printing Office, 1867). Commonly referred to as the "Doolittle Report" of 1867 for Senator James R. Doolittle, chair of the committee who prepared the report.
89. *Report of the Commissioner of Indian Affairs to the Secretary of the Interior.* (Washington, D.C.: Government Printing Office 1872) 72.
90. Ibid., 57.
91. Gale Toensing, "Indian-Killer Andrew Jackson Deserves Top Spot on List of Worst U.S. Presidents." *Indian Country Today Media Network*. 2012.
92. Ibid., 71.
93. Anne Waters, "Introduction: Indigenous Women in the Americas," *Hypatia* 18.2 (2003): xviii.
94. Smith, *Conquest.*
95. See generally: Smith, *Conquest*; Deer, "Sovereignty of the Soul"; Mihesuah, *Indigenous American Women*; Waters, "Introduction"; and Weaver, "The Colonial Context."
96. Smith, *Conquest* 79–108.
97. Ibid., 109–118.
98. Inés Hernández-Avila, "In Praise of Insubordination, Or, What Makes a Good Woman Go Bad?," *Chicana Cultural Studies Reader*, ed. Angie Chabram-Dernersesian (New York: Routledge, 2006) 198.
99. Gray, "Protecting Indian Women."

CHAPTER FIVE

Examining the Federal Response to Jurisdictional Conflicts in Indian Country: The Tribal Law and Order Act of 2010

> I know that too often, this community has heard grand promises from Washington that turned out to be little more than empty words. And I pledged to you then that if you gave me a chance, this time it would be different.
>
> —PRESIDENT BARACK OBAMA AT THE SIGNING OF THE TRIBAL LAW AND ORDER ACT[1]

On May 15, 1994, Lisa Marie Iyotte (Lakota) was brutally beaten and raped on the Rosebud Indian Reservation. She went to an Indian Health Services hospital to receive treatment for her injuries, but no doctors talked to her about her rape. Federal authorities did not interview her. Ms. Iyotte wanted to pursue her case, but federal attorneys declined to prosecute it. The man who attacked her went on to assault another woman and rape a teenage girl before he was finally arrested. He was never charged for the assault and rape of Ms. Iyotte.[2]

Sixteen years later, Lisa Iyotte found herself at the White House sharing her story in front of a national audience. In a devastating speech, Ms. Iyotte described the way that she was systematically denied justice in a society that let her case "fall through the cracks."[3] However, she remained hopeful that future legislation could help women like her find justice. As Ms. Iyotte concluded her speech, she introduced President Barack Obama who proceeded to sign the Tribal Law and Order Act of 2010 into law. At the signing, President Obama recognized the epidemic of sexual violence against Native women in Indian country stating, "when one in three Native American women will be raped in their lifetimes, that is an assault on our national conscience; it is an affront to our shared humanity; it is something that we cannot allow to continue," and that despite a history of empty promises from the federal government, "this time it would be different."[4]

The Tribal Law and Order Act of 2010 (TLOA) is the result of advocacy from both Native and non-Native community organizations and individuals, as well as media attention from organizations like Amnesty International.[5] Hailed as an astounding victory by many,[6] the TLOA is the first comprehensive bill aimed at addressing jurisdictional conflicts in Indian country with a focus on addressing sexual violence against Native women. While most non-Native sources applaud the TLOA as "a huge victory for human rights,"[7] some in the Native community are reserved in their celebration of this new law. Highlighting the apparent contradiction of using federal Indian law to fix a problem created by federal Indian policy, many Native women problematize the Act. While the TLOA is variably supported and opposed by those in the Native community, many Native women conceptualize the TLOA as an important "step in the right direction" that will take continued advocacy to perfect. This chapter examines the ways that the TLOA addresses jurisdictional conflicts in Indian country as well as the way it is conceptualized by the Native community. In doing so, I measure the TLOA against a master narrative of federal Indian policy in order to discuss if—as President Obama promised—this time it will indeed be different.

Framing the Problem, Framing Solutions

This research demonstrates that jurisdictional conflicts are part of a master narrative of federal Indian policy characterized by divestments in Native sovereignty and investments in American hegemony. Here, even when trying to solve perceived issues in Indian country, the federal government often exacerbates problems for Native people by continuing to colonize Native justice systems. Public Law 280 is just one of many examples demonstrating that when legislation to address law and order in Indian country is done in a way that divests in tribal sovereignty, it may exacerbate the problem it is trying to solve, creating even more problems in Native communities. Keen attention to the TLOA is therefore vital as it can indicate if the federal government has broken with its tradition of compounding problems in Indian country. By measuring the TLOA against the backdrop of federal Indian policy that I have developed, while incorporating the perspectives of Native women and Native communities, we can begin to contemplate the possibility of legislating a solution to jurisdictional conflicts and sexual violence in Indian country in a way that both invests in and enfranchises Native communities. To do this, I examine the way that the TLOA frames problems and solutions to sexual violence in Indian country, as well as its efficacy as articulated by Native women and nations.

Though jurisdictional conflicts have been operating in the lives of Native people in Indian country for over a century, the extreme nature of this problem has only recently reached larger audiences. Though Native people have been lobbying members of Congress for decades to draft legislation to address this issue, it wasn't until the Amnesty International report *Maze of Injustice* was released in 2007 that lawmakers crafted such legislation in the form of the TLOA. In creating *Maze*, Amnesty International—a non-Native human rights organization—worked actively with Native women and Native community organizations to draft a Native-centered report. From this initial collaborative project, media outlets like National Public Radio, *The Denver Post*, and Current TV began publishing information on sexual violence against Native women in Indian country.[8] Increased awareness of the issue outside of Native communities helped pressure Congress to take action, and on July 29, 2010, the TLOA was signed into law.

Major findings identified in the Act include: rates of sexual violence against women are extremely high in Indian country; jurisdictional conflicts negatively impact public safety in Indian country, and these conflicts have been exploited by criminals; and tribal justice systems are "often the most appropriate institutions for maintaining law and order in Indian country."[9] To address these findings, the major goals of the TLOA are to: increase coordination between federal, state and tribal entities; empower tribal governments; and reduce the prevalence of sexual violence against Native women.[10]

In order to achieve these goals, the Act takes several approaches: grant making to tribal governments; information sharing between tribal, state and federal entities; implementing standardized procedures for data and evidence collection; creating new federal liaison positions; and increasing tribal sentencing authority.[11] The TLOA makes large grants available for Native nations to enhance their tribal justice systems by providing funding for the hiring and training of new police officers, the purchase of new equipment such as computers, weapons and vehicles, and the construction of detention facilities. To facilitate information sharing, the TLOA establishes a program where Native nations may gain access to national crime databases. Additionally, the TLOA requires the Department of Justice to publish declination rates for crimes originating in Indian country and improves the collection of reservation crime data in general. The TLOA implements standardized procedures in Indian Health Service facilities to respond to sexual assault cases and also requires specialized "family violence" training for law enforcement officers and prosecutors to better work with Native survivors. The TLOA also establishes the Office of Tribal Justice and creates several new federal positions and committees that work to facilitate communication between the federal, state and tribal governments when handling cases that originate in Indian country. Furthermore, the TLOA allows Native nations in PL 280 states to call on the federal government when state governments do not adequately address crimes that originate in Indian country. And finally, the TLOA expands tribal sentencing authority to up to three years in jail and up to a $15,000 fine for any single offense (up from one year and $5,000 since the Indian Civil Rights Act was amended in 1986).[12]

The TLOA represents an important point of departure from the dominant narrative of federal Indian policy. Breaking from its decidedly non-democratic tradition of excluding Native people from creating the legislation that would then control their lives, members of Congress actively worked with Native leaders to craft the TLOA. Representative Herseth Sandlin from South Dakota and Senator Byron Dorgan from North Dakota convened several Senate committee meetings to hear from Native representatives about how they conceptualized problems and solutions to jurisdictional conflicts and sexual violence against Native women in Indian country.[13] Unlike the vast majority of federal Indian policy, the TLOA marks a distinct shift in that it begins to incorporate Native voices into the legislation that directly affects Native communities. This Native-centered shift in thinking is further indicated by the Act itself that requires many federal agencies to act "in consultation" with Native nations when making decisions about law enforcement in Indian country.[14]

While this may represent an important break from earlier federal policy, we must problematize the way that Native people were variously included and excluded from this process. While consultation with Native people marks an improvement from a tradition of deciding what is best for Native people without asking them, the Act fails at truly giving agency to Native communities themselves. Despite the TLOA's insistence that its goal is to "empower tribal governments [...] to safely and effectively provide public safety in Indian country,"[15] the federal government still had the final say in the authorship of this Act. The TLOA was written by non-Native legislators and was passed in a Congress with only one member who is enrolled in a Native nation.[16] While perhaps more familiar with the needs of Native nations through consulting certain Native leaders, Native communities did not shape this legislation in a way that truly reflects tribal sovereignty. As *Indian Country Today* recognized, "Much of the impact of the TLOA will be lost in bureaucratic regulations and administration if tribal communities and leaders do not have significant voice in the planning and organization of justice programs."[17] Whereas the TLOA offers mere consultation with a handful of Native leaders, a true method to empower tribal communities could have included joint or co-authorship of the bill by members of Native nations selected by the communities themselves.

Concern over complicated bureaucracy is frequently expressed in the Native community regarding the TLOA. One of the cornerstones of the TLOA is increased collection of reservation crime statistics as well as the publication of federal declination reports for crimes that originate in Indian country. While these statistics have been much sought after by Native women and Native communities who want to leverage them to draw attention to the problem of sexual violence against Native women, if the compilation of these statistics is not coupled with attention to the issues that produce sexual violence against Native women, this approach will do little to create meaningful change. As Carrie Garrow, Chief Judge of the St. Regis Mohawk Tribe noted, "Endless bureaucracy and more data collection is a way of *not* dealing with the problem" (emphasis in original).[18] Essentially, reporting how many cases are declined is not an effective measure to ensure that cases are prosecuted since compiling statistics and declination reports do nothing to address sexual violence at its source.

While "consulting" Native nations may be a step in the right direction, the Act does little to make Native nations full partners in the law. Again, though Native nations are to be "consulted" as the law is implemented, many of the aspects of the law that involve coordinating Native people do not actually involve Native people. For example, a central tenet of the TLOA is facilitating the adjudication of crimes that occur in Indian country between the federal, state, and tribal governments. To do this, the TLOA establishes the Office of Tribal Justice and creates several liaison positions to increase communication between these entities. Unfortunately, these positions are to be filled by assistant U.S. attorneys appointed by the U.S. attorney in each district that includes Indian country.[19] Rather than providing for Native nations to appoint their own liaisons that represent their nation's best interests, the TLOA insists on appointing more U.S. attorneys who may not be in touch with the needs of the Native community in that area, or accountable to the Native communities that they serve. Again, while creating these positions and consulting with Native nations may be seen as an improvement, it still highlights a common theme: while the federal government may intend to incorporate Native people in crafting solutions in Indian country, it continues to insist on centering itself in the formation and maintenance of these solutions.

Additionally, many Native women have called the funding for the Act into question. While the TLOA ostensibly makes millions of dollars available for Native nations to invest in their tribal justice systems, many remain skeptical as to whether or not this funding will actually become available. As Kimberly Craven

(Sisseton–Wahpeton Oyate) writes in an editorial in the *Indian Country Times*, "It is critical that Congress also appropriate the money that is needed to implement this law. Until that is done, these are probably just words on a piece of paper."[20] Virgil Wade, a criminal defender in the Salt River Pima-Maricopa Indian Community says, "I don't know that it has the teeth that it's going to need," referring to the fact that the funds to pay for the TLOA aren't guaranteed.[21] The skepticism towards fund allocation is warranted. For example, as Muskogee activist Sarah Deer points out, the Tribal Justice Act of 1993 was supposed to provide over fifty million dollars *per year* for tribal justice systems, yet when the act expired seven years later, only five million dollars had been appropriated *in total*.[22]

Appropriating funds for the TLOA can be problematic, not only because funding for the Act is not guaranteed, but also because, as with all federal grants, tribal nations must apply for them. This places Native nations in a position where they must meet certain—and often hegemonic—standards for fund allocation. While the TLOA does allow funds to be used for "alternatives to incarceration," the Act dedicates a large part of its funding towards the construction of new juvenile and adult detention facilities.[23] Other sections of the Act authorize grants for the purchase of police equipment such as weapons.[24] In this way, funding for Native nations is framed in terms of increased resources for Western-style law-and-order systems that value punishment and incarceration, along with increased police presence to guarantee safety. As Native activist Jessica Yee (Mohawk) notes:

> A thing that somewhat troubles me about the bill is a lot [sic] on criminalization and penalization. I'm a prison abolitionist in many senses and I'm very aware of how many Indigenous people are in the criminal justice system unfairly; but more importantly, that these entire systems are not our laws and not our systems.[25]

Here, many Native women agree that increased state violence will not help eradicate violence caused by the state. As one Native woman so succinctly noted, "We can't arrest our way out of this problem."[26]

Western Legal Hegemony

In addition to increased funding for police weaponry and detention facilities, the TLOA grants Native nations greater authority to make arrests, sentence perpetrators, and access national criminal databases. This is important because tribal police will now be able to run background checks to determine if someone is a convicted criminal or sex offender. However, access to these systems is predicated on tribal police becoming "consistent with standards" accepted by the federal government.[27] In other words, tribal police must subscribe to hegemonic standards of Western law enforcement procedures in order to have access to this vital information. Furthermore, while the Act encourages agreements between tribal law enforcement officers and local police, this is at the discretion of the attorney general who "may provide technical and other assistance to state, tribal, and local governments" to enter into "mutual aid, hot pursuit of suspects, and cross-deputization agreements."[28] While the TLOA is ostensibly about encouraging cooperation between the federal, state, and tribal entities, it does so with a top-down approach by appointing attorneys and federal liaisons to oversee relationships, rather than directly addressing cooperation on an everyday level. And the only section of the Act to directly address coordination between tribal and local police dictates that it will be at the attorney general's discretion. Here, the only way that tribal police officers may arrest non-Native assailants is through entering into a cross-deputization agreement with local authorities. Cross-deputization has been problematized by many Native women, notably Eileen Luna-Firebaugh (Choctaw/Cherokee), who notes that they force tribal police to adhere to Western legal standards in order to be seen as legitimate by local authorities.[29] In order for tribal police to exercise even a modified form of jurisdictional and local control under the TLOA, non-Native law enforcement officers must train and certify them. Here non-Native law enforcement agencies are modeled as ideal, thereby implying the inferiority of Native justice systems.

In addition to forcing Native nations to ascribe to Western notions of justice, the way that the TLOA structures sentencing authority is an example of the ubiquitous fear of Native justice systems that structures federal Indian policy. In 1968, the federal government imposed mandatory sentencing restrictions on tribal governments under the Indian Civil Rights Act of 1968 (ICRA).[30] Stemming from federal paternalism to protect Native people from their own governments, the ICRA initially limited tribal governments to imposing sentences of no more than six months in jail and a $500 fine per offense on those who were convicted in tribal court. The TLOA increased these limitations to three years and $15,000 respectively.[31] However, in order to hand down sentences in excess of one year and a $5,000 fine, the Tribal Law and Order Act states that a tribal court must provide the defendant with counsel "at least equal to that guaranteed by the United States Constitution," who is licensed to practice law in the United States, and that the judge presiding over the trial must also be licensed in the United States. All of this must be "at the expense of the tribal government."[32] Not only do sentencing limitations indicate the federal perception that Native people must be protected from their own governments, but the fact that in order to even operate within these limitations tribal nations must also subscribe to Western hegemonic systems of justice, demonstrates that the federal government clearly does not intend to invest in tribal sovereignty in a meaningful way. As one Native woman in an *Indian Country Today* editorial blog observed:

> This piece of legislation contains sections that once again diminish tribal sovereignty! Tribes can only increase incarceration IF they provide certain protections for defendants. Specifically, judges and public defenders must be lawyers. Also, they must follow American legal procedures. Not all tribes currently provide these types of services in their tribal court systems, neither do they have the resources to comply with these requirements. Once again, another example of the guardian ward relationship being reinforced [emphasis in original].[33]

Another woman, identifying as Turtle Mountain Ojibwe observed:

> I applaude [sic] the passing of the new Law and Order Act for Indian country, however after reading through the act more carefully, discovered that in order for tribes to pass and enact this new Bill we once again lost more of our sovereignty. According to this ACT [sic], tribes who decide to implement this new Law and Order Act are required to follow State law and court procedures, rather then [sic] tribal laws and court procedures. Just one more example of the Federal Government taking our rights away in the disguise of helping, what a shame, but to be expected.[34]

In these quotes, Native women problematize the relationship between the federal government and Native nations as one that has been marked by paternalism and attacks on tribal sovereignty. Again, we see the common theme that Native governments become legitimate only when they become more like the hegemonic ideal of Western government. Despite stating that tribal justice systems are the best place to adjudicate crimes in Indian country, the TLOA frames them as effective only when these systems are shaped to mirror American models. Additionally, the fact that tribes are forced to pay the cost of conforming to Western justice systems leads many Native women to refer to the TLOA as an "unfunded mandate."[35] Furthermore, there is a provision under the increased sentencing section of the TLOA that describes how after four years the attorney general will recommend, "whether enhanced sentencing authority should be discontinued, enhanced, or maintained at the level authorized under this title."[36] In other words, once the federal government determines whether or not tribes have been "effective"[37] in their use of enhanced sentencing laws, the federal government will paternalistically decide whether or not they should be allowed to continue to have increased sentencing authority.

As Chapter Three demonstrated, federal law and policy has sought to manage the "Indian problem" by delivering Native people out of savagery and into civilization. So far we have seen how the TLOA views "strengthening tribal justice systems" as synonymous with using federal funding to force tribal justice systems to mirror Western government, and that after a period of time the federal government will assess whether or not tribal governments can be trusted with increased responsibility. This not only reveals a paternal narrative, but also a civilizing one. From a federal perspective, the TLOA's efficacy is framed in part through its potential to create competency in tribal justice institutions through federal intervention. This by definition assumes the inherent *in*competency of tribal justice as it exists now, and places the TLOA on the colonial legal trajectory of using federal Indian policy to manage the "Indian problem" through Western law as a civilizing force.

Assimilation as part of the civilizing project of federal Indian policy is found throughout the non-Native legislative discourse around the TLOA. Rather than framing sexual violence as the direct result of colonization and the formation of the United States, sexual violence originating in Indian country is often divorced from its colonial context. Framed paternalistically in terms of delivering Native people into the safety of the America dream, the rhetoric around the TLOA is characterized by phrases such as all Native people deserve to enjoy the "fullest protection of *our* laws,"[38] (my emphasis) and that "every American has the right to live in a safe community," even our "First Americans."[39] At the 2009 Tribal Nations Conference where he announced his support for the TLOA, President Obama emphasized his commitment to the nation-to-nation relationship between Native nations and the federal government so that tribes can "be full partners in the American economy, and so your children and grandchildren can have an equal shot at pursuing the American Dream."[40] While this type of rhetoric may sound pro-Indian, it fails to be truly pro-sovereignty. As many Native scholars point out, the American economy could not have been built without the colonization of Native people, and as such, realizing the "American Dream" is not always a goal of Native peoples.[41] Additionally, framing the TLOA as something that gives Native people the fullest protection of American laws demonstrates the failure of the federal government to understand that federal laws have actually *created* the impunity through which Native women are preyed upon in Indian country. What many in the Native community are demanding is not equal protection *under* American law, but the right to protect themselves *from* American law, through self-determination and sovereignty over their own lands, laws, and justice systems.

Additionally, many in the Native community are skeptical of being forced to adopt a Western justice model that appears to be dysfunctional by its own standards. As noted in Chapter One, Cherokee scholar Andrea Smith argues that the Western criminal justice system generally functions at the point of crisis *after* violence has occurred.[42] And Sarah Deer (Muscogee Creek) notes, "I'm always concerned about 'law and order' language. It certainly doesn't protect or help white women, so it's not going to help Native women. We have to make sure that the systems we set up are Native women-centered."[43] Full inclusion and equal protection under the law of the very institution that has divested Native people of their lands and resources are not necessarily the goals of Native communities. While the federal government may continue its mission to deliver Native people into civilization by incorporating them into American legal hegemony, Native communities articulate solutions in terms of sovereignty and centering Native women in their anti-violence strategies.

The Homogenization of Violence: Racial Identity and Predatory Violence

As this chapter indicates, while the TLOA is framed as being liberatory for Native people, it is in fact deeply hegemonic and fits within a narrative of federal paternalism. Yet this analysis stands apart from what is by far the most problematic aspect of the TLOA. Despite admitting that "tribal nations are the best place to handle issues of tribal law and order," and despite the fact that specific pieces of federal Indian law and policy have clearly created jurisdictional conflicts, the TLOA does absolutely nothing to address these policies or address the dynamics of interracial violence that characterize the majority of sexual assault against Native women.

The TLOA specifically acknowledges that more than one in three Native women will be raped in her lifetime and that violence against Native women is 2.5 times that of the national average.[44] American politicians quote these statistics in virtually every speech as they pledge their support of the TLOA. But despite being published in many of the same reports that reveal these startling facts, one statistic you will not find in federal political discourse is the fact that while rape is an overwhelmingly intra-racial crime in the United States, 86% of Native women who are raped report that their attacker is a non-Native man, 80% of whom are white. If politicians were to acknowledge that interracial rape is rare in non-Native communities yet routine for Native women, they would be forced to address the history that has created these disparate statistics. However, doing so would require a discussion of American colonization and is thus inconvenient to the settler-state. As such, the interracial aspect of sexual violence and jurisdictional conflicts is never addressed. While truly addressing jurisdictional conflicts would mean crafting legislation that bolsters a Native nation's ability to address *all* violence against Native women, the TLOA instead focuses on strengthening tribal policing of the mere 14% of *intra*-racial sexual assault in Indian country. In ignoring the inter-racial aspect of sexual violence against Native women by racing the perpetrators of violence in Indian country as Native, the TLOA both strengthens tribal justice systems to police and incarcerate their own Native people disproportionately while continuing to deny Native nations the authority to exercise control over those who commit the vast majority of sexual assault against Native women.

One of the cornerstones of the TLOA is "strengthening tribal justice systems," accomplished primarily through increased funding for policing and prisons. However, because the Tribal Law and Order Act does not overturn *Oliphant*, all of the funding that would go to tribal governments under the TLOA would—by definition—only be used to police Native people. Here, all of the federal money used to "strengthen tribal justice systems" would specifically go to prosecuting and incarcerating Native people exclusively. As Native scholar Luana Ross points out, the criminalization of Native identity and legacies of historical trauma have led to an astounding over-representation of Native people in the criminal justice system as it is.[45] The TLOA would then only invest in tribal justice systems to the extent that they might further police and jail their own members, while doing little to address the root causes and realities of sexual violence against Native women.

Despite the fact that virtually every scholar points to federal Indian policy like the Major Crimes Act, the Dawes Act, Public Law 280 and *Oliphant v. Suquamish* as the cause of jurisdictional conflicts in Indian country, the TLOA refuses to address them. In fact, the Act *protects* and *strengthens* pre-existing law and policy by amending the Indian Civil Rights Act and by explicitly protecting the ruling in *Oliphant*. Without mentioning the case by name, Section 206 removes any doubt over the TLOA's impact on *Oliphant* by stating, "Nothing in this Act confers on an Indian tribe criminal jurisdiction over non-Indians."[46] In doing so, Section 206 affirms *Oliphant* as case law and reiterates the federal government's position that state and/or federal entities are the true arbiters of justice for the majority of crimes committed against Native women in Indian country.

Because the TLOA explicitly protects the root causes of jurisdictional conflicts, it can never adequately address them. Instead, the TLOA appears to be another case of legislating over the problem, rather than addressing it directly. This fits neatly into the master narrative of federal policy in which the government enacts a series of reactive policies out of a fear of Native justice systems, rather than meaningfully investing in these systems. As Native women and Native communities conceptualize the TLOA, they often comment on this tendency. For example, Diane Enos, president of the Salt River Pima-Maricopa Indian Community in Arizona, states of the TLOA, "You've got Congress people scared stiff of seeing tribes get authority over non-Indians. I'm not sure that they understand why, but it's almost a knee-jerk reaction."[47] As Native activist Sarah Deer notes of the passage of the TLOA:

> I should just be satisfied with celebrating this victory, but I'd really like to see Congress take on this issue of non-Indian perpetrators [...] I think there's a fear that tribal governments will be harsher on non-Indians. I think that's a racist idea at its core [...] the idea that tribal people can't be fair. If you take racism out of the picture, then what the rule is doesn't make sense.[48]

Both Deer and Enos's statements frame true solutions to jurisdictional conflicts and sexual violence in terms of investments in tribal sovereignty, while positioning the TLOA as reactive to the fear of Native justice systems. Noting the reactionism and fear that characterizes aspects of the TLOA, Native women and Native community members consistently incorporate an analysis of sovereignty into their perceptions of the TLOA. As Rose from South Dakota comments in *Indian Country Today*:

> I feel confident the tribes can handle their own affairs and what would happen if we went to Senator Dorgan's home state and tried to enforce a law upon the citizens? It's so tragic for the Indian Nations. This is just another pretext of repressive policy and example of the guardian-ward relationship.[49]

Furthermore, Tsoo'woo Naibi comments in *Indian Country Today*:

> We are a strong people whose heritage is based on a balance between individual autonomy and strong community ties. We still have the power to achieve this, and can better achieve it if the U.S. steps out of our affairs.[50]

At the Tribal Nations Conference of 2009 when President Obama announced his intentions to sign the TLOA, he stated, "I believe that Washington can't—and shouldn't—dictate a policy agenda for Indian country. Tribal nations do better when they make their own decisions. That's why we're here today."[51] Yet one is left to wonder if a TLOA that purports to invest in tribal justice systems, and notes that tribes are the best institutions to maintain law and order in Indian country, actually incorporates the kind of self-determination that President Obama claims to support. At every turn Native women and Native communities articulate that sovereignty and self-determination is absolutely vital in shaping a better future for themselves. Yet the TLOA insists on continuing to invest in the "guardian"/"ward" relationship codified in the 1830s that defined Native people as child-like "wards"[52] of the paternal federal government.

Like federal Indian policy before it, the TLOA acts out of a colonial fear of the inferiority of tribal justice systems and paternalistically dictates the ways in which Native nations may exert authority over the people and activities on their land while increasing state violence against Native people through policing and incarceration. Despite President Obama's promise that "this time it would be different," it appears that the TLOA still embodies many of the problems of traditional federal Indian policy that sought to manage the "Indian problem" by divesting in Native sovereignty and investing in American hegemony. While the Act reveals an understanding of the issue that is congruent with the findings of this research—that sexual violence against Native women in Indian country has reached epidemic proportions and that jurisdictional conflicts play a major role in this violence—the solutions proposed in the TLOA do little to address the problem at its core. Instead, the federal government continues to vest federal and state authorities—often the most distant, unresponsive, and unaccountable entities—with jurisdictional authority over crimes in Indian country. At the same time, the interracial aspect of sexual assault is erased, as the federal government refuses to acknowledge its role in the creation and maintenance of these conflicts.

Despite the obvious shortcomings of this Act, it would be a mistake to universally condemn it. In spite of its limitations, Native women and Native organizations also offer praise of the TLOA. Native women like Lisa Iyotte, whose story we heard at the beginning of this chapter, describe how this act can help prevent cases from "falling through the cracks." Jessica Yee, a Native blogger for Ms. Magazine stated "As a Native feminist without apology, I'm thrilled that the Tribal Law and Order Act of 2010 has been passed to protect Native women from violence."[53] Other Native women have stated "I think now the women finally have a voice [...] I sit with women who cry and are mad because the feds didn't want to pick up the case. This bill, I think, would give women more of a right [...]"[54] These statements do not come as a result of ignorance of the true content of the Act, but instead support for the TLOA comes from a willingness to engage in what Chela Sandoval refers to as a "differential consciousness."

In *Methodology of the Oppressed*, Sandoval argues that social movements are often framed with an either/or approach of choosing one organizing strategy over another.[55] In the either/or paradigm, organizing within competing power structures often positions women as having to choose between adversarial approaches to social change. However, what Sandoval engages in *Methodology* is the idea that women of color can and do negotiate seemingly oppositional power structures, refusing to choose one or the other. Instead, they strategically navigate opposing spaces with a willingness to engage in multiple approaches even if these approaches may at first appear to conflict.[56] She refers to this type of consciousness as a "differential" in that it "enables movement 'between and among' ideological positionings."[57] Much like a transmission differential in a car, activists can shift between different approaches in the face of changing terrain to strategically navigate contemporary institutions to shape a better world for themselves and their communities. So rather than completely embrace the TLOA as the ultimate solution to sexual violence and jurisdictional conflicts, or alternatively reject the TLOA as worthless because it fails to frame solutions in ways that are truly liberating for Native communities, Native women invoke a differential consciousness to leverage the potential benefits of the TLOA while also acknowledging and addressing its shortcomings.

We see differential consciousness employed by many Native women as they discuss the TLOA. As Nicole Mathews (White Earth Ojibwe), executive director of the Minnesota Indian Women's Sexual Assault Coalition stated, "I think that the Obama administration has really taken some great steps to improve safety for Native women in Native country [...] But there is more work ahead. Now we have to take steps to make it a reality."[58] Lucy Simpson (Navajo) an attorney for the Indian Law Resource Center continues, "The Tribal Law and Order Act that Obama just passed provides a little step in the right direction."[59] Muscogee activist Sarah Deer states, "[T]his took three years. It's really been 500 years, but three years of putting it on paper. There are ten or twelve more steps we need to do, of course, but now it feels like we can change the world." She goes on to say, "This [Act] is a very, very tiny beginning, but now I really believe it can be done. I don't know if I will see it in my lifetime, but I'm committed to making sure I do the work anyway."[60] In another piece, she also states, "I see the [TLOA] as a foundation [...] I worry sometimes that people expect a 'quick fix' to problems that have been ongoing for over a century. While the TLOA didn't contain all the fixes (or dollars) that would be ideal, we now have a starting point."[61]

By invoking a differential consciousness, Native women conceptualize the TLOA, not as a "quick fix," but instead as a framework from which they can base future activism both within *and* outside of existing institutions. These Native women acknowledge that there is still much more work to be done, but rather than reject a piece of legislation because it is problematic, they are willing to strategically leverage it to shape a better future. While many acknowledge that solutions to sexual violence in Indian country will likely not come from the very government that has consistently inscribed violence on Indian people, it doesn't necessarily preclude Native activists from using each potential asset as they work to create a world that is safe for Native women. And, as we look at other sites of activism, this ability to invoke a differential consciousness becomes central to framing solutions to jurisdictional conflicts and sexual violence.

Notes

1. Barack Obama. "Remarks By the President Before Signing the Tribal Law and Order Act." Office of the Press Secretary. The White House. 29 Jul. 2010. Print.
2. Lisa Iyotte. "Remarks Before Signing of the Tribal Law and Order Act." The White House. Washington, D.C. Video. 29 Jul. 2010. <http://www.whitehouse.gov/blog/2010/07/29/tribal-law-and-order-act-2010-a-step-forward-native-women> Accessed 12 Apr. 2011.
3. Ibid.
4. Obama, "Remarks by the President."
5. Non-Native advocates include Representative Herseth-Sandlin of South Dakota, Senator Byron Dorgan of North Dakota, the American Bar Association, and Amnesty International. Native advocates include Sarah Deer and Native community organizations like the Qualla Women's Justice Alliance, Strong Hearted Native Women's Coalition, Inc., and Mending the Sacred Hoop Technical Assistance Project. See Congressional Senate Hearing, "Examining S. 797, The Tribal Law and Order Act of 2009," 111th Congress. First Session. (Washington, D.C.: GPO, 2009) Print.
6. See for example Angela Chang of Amnesty International, "Victory! Tribal Law and Order Act Passes in the US Senate!" *Amnesty International USA Web Log*. Web. 1 Jul. 2010. <http://blog.amnestyusa.org/women/victory-tribal-law-and-order-act-passes-in-the-us-senate/> Jul 1 2010> Accessed 12 Apr. 2011.
7. Ibid.
8. See the work of Laura Sullivan of National Public Radio, Michael Riley of *Denver Post* and Current TV's *Vanguard* documentary "Rape on the Reservation" Jun. 2010.
9. Tribal Law and Order Act. Pub L. No 111-211. 29 Jul. 2010. Sec. 202.a.1–7.
10. Ibid., 202.b.1–6.
11. Tribal Law and Order Act.
12. Ibid.
13. See for example Senate Committee hearing *Examining S. 797*.
14. The TLOA uses the phrase "in consultation with Indian tribes" throughout the Act. See for example Sec 211.f.3, Sec 231.b.i.
15. Tribal Law and Order Act. Sec. 202.b.3.
16. Representative Tom Cole (Chickasaw) of Oklahoma's 4th district was the only member of the 111th Congress enrolled in a federally recognized tribe. ("111th Congress: Statistically Speaking," *CQ Today*. 6 Nov. 2008. Web. Accessed 12 Apr. 2011 <www.cq.com/graphics/monitor/.../mon20081105-5election-stats.pdf>
17. "Our Input Still Needed in Law and Order Act," *Indian Country Today*. Web. 2 Sep. 2010. <http://www.indiancountrytoday.com/internal?st=print&id=102101183&path=/opinion.editorials> Accessed 12 Apr. 2010.
18. As quoted in Mac McClelland, "A Fistful of Dollars," *Mother Jones* Nov-Dec. 2010: 65.
19. Tribal Law and Order Act. Sec. 13.a.
20. Article comment by Kimberley Craven, 30 Jul. 2010 in Gale Toensing, "Obama Signs 'Historic' Tribal Law and Order Act." *Indian Country Today*. Web. 30 Jul. 2010. <http://www.indiancountrytoday.com/home/content/Obama-signs-historic-Tribal-Law-and-Order-Act-99620099.html> Accessed 12 Apr. 2011.

21. McClelland, "Fistful of Dollars."
22. Deer, "Federal Indian Law and Violent Crime" 40.
23. Tribal Law and Order Act. Sec. 211.f.1.c.
24. "Summary of the Tribal Law and Order Act." United States Senate Committee on Indian Affairs. Mar. 2009. Web. Accessed 4 Oct. 2010. <www.indian.senate.gov/public/_files/TLOonepagerMar2009.pdf>
25. Jessica Yee, "How Native Women Built the Tribal Law and Order Act," *Ms. Magazine Blog* Web. 3 Aug. 2010. <http://msmagazine.com/blog/blog/2010/08/03/the-woman-behind-the-tribal-law-and-order-act> Accessed 12 Apr. 2011.
26. Pember, "Tribes Gain New Clout."
27. Tribal Law and Order Act. Sec. 231.a.1.B.i.
28. Ibid. Sec. 222.
29. Luna-Firebaugh, *Tribal Policing* 40.
30. The Indian Civil Rights Act (ICRA) of 1968 imposes many of the amendments in the U.S. Bill of Rights onto Native nations. While framed as benevolently granting the full protection of American laws to Native peoples, the ICRA inscribed Western hegemonic justice systems in Native communities. See Steven Pevar as quoted in Deer, "Federal Indian Law and Violent Crime" 35.
31. Tribal Law and Order Act. Sec. 234.C.
32. Ibid., Sec. 234.b.1–3.
33. Article comment by Honorindians, 31 Jul. 2010 in Toensing, "Obama Signs 'Historic' Tribal Law and Order Act."
34. Article comment by J. Charette (Turtle Mountain Ojibwe), 31 Jul. 2010. Ibid.
35. See for example Rosa Maria Cortez, senior attorney with the Navajo Nation: "We see [the TLOA] as an unfunded mandate." From "Tribes Question 'Unfunded Mandate' From Tribal Law and Order Act," *indianz.com* Web. 27 Aug. 2010. <http://64.38.12.138/News/2010/021398.asp accessed> Accessed 12 Apr. 2011.
36. Tribal Law and Order Act. Sec. 234.b.2.
37. Ibid., Sec. 234.b.1.
38. Obama stated that by passing the TLOA "I intend to send a clear message that all of our people—whether they live in our biggest cities or our most remote reservations—have the right to feel safe in their own communities, and to raise their children in peace, and enjoy the fullest protection of our laws." From Obama, "Remarks By the President."
39. Quoting Senator Byron Dorgan in Rob Capriccioso, "Tribal Law and Order Act Costly," *Tribune Business News* 28 Jul. 2010.
40. Remarks of President Obama at the White House Tribal Nations Conference of 2009. From Kimberly Teehee, "Forging a New and Better Future Together," Office of Public Engagement. The White House. Web. 21 Jul. 2010. <http://www.whitehouse.gov/blog/2010/06/21/forging-a-new-and-better-future> Accessed 12 Apr. 2011.
41. See for example the work of Haunani-Kay Trask, e.g. "Settlers of Color and 'Immigrant' Hegemony: 'Locals' in Hawai'i." *Amerasia Journal*. UCLA Asian American Studies Center Press. 26.2 (2000): 1–24.
42. Smith, *Conquest*. 169.
43. Yee, "How Native Women Built the Tribal Law and Order Act."

44. Tribal Law and Order Act. Sec. 202.
45. Ross, *Inventing the Savage.*
46. Tribal Law and Order Act. Sec. 206.
47. Jenny Gold, "Bill Bolsters Tribal Power to Prosecute Rape Cases," *National Public Radio*. 23 Jul. 2008.
48. Paul Schmelzer, "Overdue Indian Crime Bill Passes Without Support of Colo. Republicans," *Colorado Independent* Web. 28 Jul. 2010. <http://coloradoindependent.com/58201/overdue-indian-crime-bill-passes-without-support-of-colo-republicans> Accessed 12 Apr 2011.
49. Article comment by Rose 30 Jul. 2010 in Toensing, "Obama Signs 'Historic' Tribal Law and Order Act."
50. Article comment by Tsoo'woo Naibi, 30 Jul. 2010. Ibid.
51. Remarks by President Barack Obama in "Forging a New and Better Future Together: 2010 White House Tribal Nations Conference Progress Report." The White House. 23 Jun. 2010. Print.
52. See specifically *Cherokee Nation v. Georgia* (1831) in which U.S. Supreme Court Chief Justice John Marshall referred to Native people as "wards" of the U.S. government. *Cherokee Nation* along with *Johnson v. M'Intosh* (1823) and *Worcester v. Georgia* (1832) comprise the "Marshall Trilogy" of Supreme Court cases that form the foundation of federal Indian policy.
53. Yee, "How Native Women Built the Tribal Law and Order Act."
54. Georgia Littleshield, director of the Pretty Bird Woman House domestic violence shelter on the Standing Rock Sioux reservation in South Dakota. Quoted in Gold, "Bill Bolsters Tribal Power to Prosecute Rape Cases."
55. Chela Sandoval, "U.S. Third World Feminism: Differential Social Movement I," *Methodology of the Oppressed* (Minneapolis: University of Minnesota Press, 2000): 40–63.
56. Sandoval, *Methodology of the Oppressed* 57–60.
57. Ibid., 57.
58. Quoted in Sheila Regan, "Tribal Law and Order Act's XI Addresses Indian Women Sexual Assault Issues," *Twin Cities Daily Planet.* Web. 27 Oct. 2010. <http://www.tcdailyplanet.net/news/2010/10/11/tribal-law-and-order-act%E2%80%99s-xi-addresses-indian-women-sexual-assault-issues> Accessed 12 Apr. 2011.
59. Quoted in Jeanette Fordyce, "Safe Women, Strong Nations Project Combats Rape on Reservations," *Twin Cities Daily Planet.* 3 Aug. 2010. Web. <http://www.tcdailyplanet.net/news/2010/08/02/safe-women-strong-nations-project> Accessed 12 Apr. 2011.
60. Quoted in Yee, "How Native Women Built the Tribal Law and Order Act."
61. Quoted in Pember, "Tribes Gain New Clout."

CHAPTER SIX

The Ghost of Kȟaŋǧí Šúŋka and the Enduring Myth of Savage Justice: The 2013 Reauthorization of the Violence Against Women Act

> Unfortunately, certain Republicans are singing the old song of unsophisticated tribal courts and uneducated tribal judges to stop the bill from going forward [...] I say, if you don't trust the ability of tribal courts to be fair and just, don't go to the reservation and rape women—but that's just my take.
>
> —INDIAN AFFAIRS ATTORNEY RYAN DREVESKRACHT[1]

In early 2013, Chuck Grassley, a Republican Senator from Iowa, held a small town hall meeting. As he addressed his constituents, he spoke about his opposition to the renewal of the recently expired Violence Against Women Act (VAWA). The VAWA had been passed in 1994 and reauthorized with bipartisan support in 2000 and 2005. Despite its past success with support from the Republican Party, in 2012 Grassley joined a cohort of Republican congressmen in voting against the reauthorization. Like many of his colleagues, Grassley's opposition focused on newly introduced language in the bill that would address violence against Native women by expanding limited criminal jurisdiction to tribal governments. Explaining his position to his audience, Grassley stated:

> [Y]ou get non-Indians going into a reservation and violating a woman. They need to be prosecuted, they aren't prosecuted, so the idea behind this bill is we'll try 'em in tribal court. But under the laws of our land, you gotta have a jury that is a reflection of a society as a whole and on a Indian reservation, it's gonna be made up of Indians, right? So the non-Indian doesn't get a fair trial [sic].[2]

Despite Republican protest, the VAWA was reauthorized and signed into law on March 7, 2013. The final version of the 2013 reauthorization includes the provisions opposed by Grassley and others in his party. These provisions, among other things, offer limited special domestic violence criminal jurisdiction to federally recognized tribes over some non-Native perpetrators who commit violence against Native women in Indian country.

This chapter analyzes the development of, opposition to, and implementation of the Violence Against Women Reauthorization Act of 2013 (VAWA 2013) with a focus on Title IX: "Safety for Indian Women" (Title IX). In doing so, I theorize VAWA 2013 from a perspective that contextualizes it in a historical narrative to discuss its potential to address jurisdictional conflicts and sexual violence against Native women in Indian country. By grounding my analysis in a discussion of Native perceptions of the law, I argue that VAWA 2013 is a watershed moment in federal Indian policy in that it frames Native sovereignty as part of the solution to violence against Native women in Indian country. Despite that, it ultimately does not break with the larger narrative of colonial legal hegemony identified in this research and therefore is an incomplete solution. Though incomplete, rather than dismissing Title IX in its entirety, I demonstrate how it can be useful when *part of* a multifaceted decolonial approach that engages a differential consciousness. As such, Title IX is a promising tool to address jurisdictional conflicts and sexual violence against Native women when strategically leveraged in the Native anti-violence movement.

To show that VAWA 2013 ultimately does not break with American colonial legal hegemony, I problematize both the outcome of the Act in its final form as a law, as well as the conservative opposition to the congressional bill. Though opponents of the bill were ultimately unsuccessful, this chapter insists on a thorough interrogation of oppositional discourse to VAWA 2013. Such analysis is vital in that it sheds light on modern ideological constructions of Native women and Native communities from the perspective of people and institutions of power, while situating these constructions in a colonial context.

To illustrate the importance of analyzing oppositional discourse, one must look no further than Chuck Grassley's town hall meeting. Here, Grassley framed his opposition to tribal sovereignty by couching his argument in the fear of Native justice systems. In a disingenuous interpretation of Title IX, Grassley relied on white anxiety over the perceived threat of Native sovereignty to sway his constituents. To make his point, Grassley used familiar racist constructions of Native people to communicate an age-old message: that Native people are incapable of managing the people and activities on their land, and to trust them with this responsibility is to threaten the safety of non-Native (read: white) Americans.

As I have demonstrated in previous chapters, the fear of Native savagery led to limitations on Native sovereignty; limitations on Native sovereignty led to jurisdictional conflicts; and jurisdictional conflicts facilitate sexual violence against Native women. Therefore, I argue that legislative solutions to jurisdictional conflicts should be framed in terms of addressing the roots of colonial legal violence by investing in Native sovereignty. Unfortunately, Grassley's argument originates from, and contributes to, the very fear that forms the foundation of this problem. Though Grassley was ultimately unsuccessful in convincing the majority of Congress, his arguments are still symptomatic of an enduring legacy in the federal government. As the next section will show, anti-Native sovereignty arguments against Title IX[3] fit neatly into the colonial narrative that is the subject of this research. In short, the Crow Dog of 1883 meets the Chuck Grassley of 2013.

Chuck Grassley and the Ghost of Kȟaŋǧí Šúŋka: Analyzing Opposition to Title IX of VAWA 2013

Since 1994, the VAWA has offered provisions that were designed to address violence against Native women. These provisions usually took the form of federal grants that could be used for a variety of purposes to address epidemic levels of violence in Indian country. As noted, what separates previous versions of the VAWA from the 2013 reauthorization is the extension of "special domestic violence criminal jurisdiction" over non-Native perpetrators of violence in Indian country.[4] This special jurisdiction covers non-Native perpetrated assault on Native victims in Indian country when: the perpetrator resides in the Indian country of the participating tribe, works in the Indian country of the participating tribe, or is a spouse, intimate partner or dating partner of an "Indian" who resides in Indian country. According to Title IX, when tribes exercise special domestic violence jurisdiction over a non-Native perpetrator, the defendant maintains a series of enumerated rights that protects them under the U.S. Constitution.[5]

Title IX of VAWA 2013 is a landmark in that it is the first major change in tribal jurisdiction over non-Native people since *Oliphant v. Suquamish* (1978) made it illegal for Native nations to adjudicate crime committed by non-Native perpetrators. The content of Title IX and the implications of these changes for tribal sovereignty and the Native anti-violence movement as a whole are thoroughly discussed later in this chapter. For now, it is important to note that while significant, these jurisdictional changes are modest in that they are very narrowly constructed and are explicitly backed by constitutional fail-safes that guarantee protection for non-Native defendants when in tribal custody.

The modesty of these changes and the explicit constitutional fail-safes were not enough to assuage the anxiety of dozens of members of Congress, many of whom noted their opposition to the VAWA as a whole rested firmly on these new tribal provisions. Opponents of additional protections argued that in bowing to special interests, Title IX of the VAWA is an unprecedented expansion of tribal sovereignty that—among other things—violates the rights of the accused. This chapter will show that from a legal perspective, this stance is unfounded. Simply reading the text of the law easily refutes many of these arguments, and a more nuanced study of federal Indian policy dismantles any lingering constitutional challenges. Despite that, many members of Congress insisted on engaging a straw person argument in an effort to curb federal investment in tribal sovereignty.

Conservative anti-Title IX arguments do not exist in a vacuum. Instead, they are a product of ideological constructions of Native people. Though couched in concern over constitutional rights, anti-VAWA arguments expose familiar fears over Native sovereignty—illustrating that white anxiety over the perceived lawlessness of Native people is still alive and well today. As this chapter will show, anti-Title IX arguments reveal historical amnesia among certain legislators who appear to ignore the U.S. Constitution and the political philosophy of the so-called founding fathers. By analyzing the subtext behind these arguments, I situate the opposition to VAWA 2013 directly within the colonial racism that has itself created jurisdictional conflicts.

Under the umbrella of "unconstitutionality," anti-Title IX arguments take many forms. Some argue that it violates states' rights,[6] but the majority insists that Title IX's limited expansion of jurisdiction is an unconstitutional extension of tribal sovereignty that denies non-Native Americans equal protection under the law. This school of thought argues that VAWA 2013 would "for the first time in the nation's history, extend criminal jurisdiction to people who are not members of an Indian tribe"[7] which is "unprecedented, unnecessary and dangerous."[8] Special domestic violence jurisdiction is framed as an "unconstitutional expansion of tribal authority"[9] that affirms the "non existent rights of self-governing bodies [i.e., Indian tribes]."[10] Sadly, those who argue that Title IX is an unconstitutional overreach, fail to acknowledge both current case law,[11] as well as the standard set forth in the U.S.'s own constitution.

At its inception, the U.S. Constitution viewed Native nations as both pre- and extra-constitutional, meaning that their sovereignty existed before that of the United States', and continues to exist outside of it.[12] This recognition of Native sovereignty is illustrated by the fact that the U.S. signed hundreds of treaties with Indian tribes—a legal process that is exclusively reserved for diplomacy with foreign nations. As noted in Chapter Three, many of these treaties included specific language guaranteeing tribal criminal jurisdiction over non-Native perpetrators in Indian Territory. In "Closing the Gap in Indian Country Justice: *Oliphant, Lara* and DOJ's Proposed Fix," author M. Brent Leonhard, deputy attorney general for the Confederated Tribes of the Umatilla Indian Reservation, takes this analysis one step further. Here, Leonhard notes that of the nine treaties that specifically acknowledge tribal jurisdiction over non-Indians in Indian Territory, six of them were ratified between 1785 and 1789 in a Congress that included thirty-three of the men who signed the U.S. Constitution.[13] This illustrates that the so-called founding fathers not only recognized inherent tribal sovereignty in general (both through language in the U.S. Constitution and through the treaty-making process), but that they also codified tribal criminal jurisdiction in particular.[14]

The fact that some legislators failed to acknowledge that even the founding fathers explicitly recognized inherent jurisdictional authority for Native nations sets the tone for subsequent arguments against Title IX. Within the trope of unconstitutionality, the most vociferous critics of Title IX allege that enhanced tribal jurisdiction violates the rights of the accused who would not be protected by the U.S. Constitution in tribal court. For example, Senator John Cornyn (R-TX) argued that VAWA 2013 is a "slippery slope because if non-tribe members are tried in tribal courts, they are not protected by the U.S. Constitution."[15] Representative Jim Sensenbrenner (R-WI) stated that Title IX, "brings huge constitutional issues because the Bill of Rights does not apply in tribal courts."[16] And conservative think tank the Heritage Foundation reported:

> Under VAWA, men effectively lose their constitutional rights to due process, presumption of innocence, equal treatment under the law, the right to a fair trial and to confront one's accusers, the right to bear arms, and all custody/visitation rights.[17]

The more radical stance against Cornyn et al. would argue that these are moot points given the doctrine of implied consent, which holds that upon entering the jurisdiction of a sovereign entity one assumes foreign jurisdiction and forfeits the protection of the United States (as when crossing the border from the United States to Canada for example). That argument aside, as the National Task Force to End Sexual and Domestic Violence Against Women points out, "the language of VAWA makes it abundantly clear that constitutional protections cannot be abridged in the process of responding to domestic violence, dating violence, sexual assault, or stalking."[18] Furthermore, as Senator Maria Cantwell (D-WA) stated on the Senate floor:

> [VAWA 2013] has specifically broad language making sure that the defendant would be protected with all rights required for [special tribal domestic violence] jurisdiction

> to have oversight. So it's almost like double protection saying twice the Habeas Corpus rights of individuals are going to be protected under this statute [sic].[19]

Not only are the rights of non-Native defendants dually established, Cantwell goes on to also note that tribal courts must also adhere to the Indian Civil Rights Act (ICRA), which guarantees all people subject to tribal governments virtually all of the protection of the U.S. Bill of Rights. In fact, as discussed in Chapter Five, the ICRA actually *limits* tribal authority over *all* defendants in tribal court. This means that not only are non-Native defendants protected by the Bill of Rights, they are also *shielded* from what could be equal to the full force of U.S. Constitutional authority itself.[20]

Title IX of VAWA 2013 was thoroughly vetted by over fifty U.S. law professors who reviewed its provisions and found them to be constitutional.[21] The text of Title IX makes it abundantly clear that non-Native defendants in tribal courts maintain a host of constitutional rights, which include the right to a public defender, the right to effective legal counsel, and the right to petition for a writ of habeas corpus.[22] Title IX also explicitly guarantees the "right to a trial by an impartial jury," which—despite its clarity—was still misrepresented by some U.S. lawmakers. As noted earlier, Chuck Grassley argued that non-Native defendants wouldn't get a fair trial under Title IX because, "under the laws of our land, you gotta have a jury that is a reflection of a society as a whole and on a Indian reservation, it's gonna be made up of Indians, right?"

On its surface, Grassley's claim is simply not true. Title IX guarantees that the right to trial includes a jury drawn from "sources that reflect a fair cross section of the community; and do not systematically exclude any distinctive group in the community, including non-Indians."[23] Additionally, there is actually no constitutional requirement that juries reflect "society as a whole." Instead, the Sixth Amendment states that juries should be drawn from the "district wherein the crime shall have been committed," and the U.S. Supreme Court later clarified that this should be, "drawn from a fair cross section of the community," where the case is tried.[24] Rather than guarantee a jury that represents America as a whole, federal law requires a jury to represent the local community in which the crime is adjudicated. As the direct result of laws like the Dawes Act, according to the 2010 U.S. census approximately 46% of people living in Indian country are non-Native, meaning that the local community in Indian country is likely to be more diverse than many cities in the United States.[25] And even if the jury did consist of all Native jurors (which, again, is illegal under Title IX), it still would not violate the "laws of our land" as Grassley stated.

Grassley's claim is notable not only because it is patently false, but because of the racist assumptions that undergird it. In misrepresenting the law, he also proffers an image of Native nations as incapable of administering justice and Native jurors as incapable of performing their civic duties as both tribal and U.S. citizens. His colleague, then Senator Kay Bailey Hutchison (R-TX), continued in this tradition arguing that Title IX "would give tribal courts authority to arrest, try and imprison *any* American" (my emphasis).[26] Hutchison's allegations imply that Native nations would arrest and imprison non-Native Americans arbitrarily. However, per VAWA 2013, Native nations only have the power to adjudicate special cases of domestic violence when perpetrators have significant ties to the community. This means they wouldn't be arresting and trying just *any* American, only community members suspected of committing a serious crime. Like Grassley, Hutchison reads Native justice as a lack of justice, one in which tribal citizens are incapable of reason and fairness and thus threaten American liberty writ large.[27]

After Chuck Grassley's town hall meeting, his spokesperson issued a statement affirming the Senator's beliefs that Title IX would violate a defendant's right to a fair trial by jury. On behalf of Grassley, she added that the U.S. Constitution guarantees "no juror be denied the right to serve based on race." According to the statement, since "[m]embership in Indian tribes is racially defined by law," a trial by tribal jury would violate the constitutional rights of Americans. A report published by the Heritage Foundation echoes this sentiment by continuing to racialize anti-sovereignty discourse stating, "American Indian tribes operate racially exclusive governments on their territories and lands," and "without precedent, [VAWA 2013] surrenders the rights of Americans who are not American Indians to racially exclusive tribal courts."[28]

Both Grassley and the Heritage Foundation fall into a familiar trap of collapsing racial, ethnic and national identities. While "American Indian" is a racial category, the term encompasses hundreds of discrete Indigenous ethnic groups who are citizens of their own sovereign nations. While it may be tempting to view tribal courts as *racially* exclusive, they are not. Instead, like the United States, they are *politically* exclusive. Though membership in federally recognized tribes does require some degree of Native ancestry, people who are phenotypically "White" or "Black" may be enrolled members along with their phenotypically "American Indian" counterparts. Conversely, people who have blood ancestry and are phenotypically "American Indian," might not be citizens because they have not enrolled or do not meet eligibility criteria for membership. It is not one's phenotypical presentation of race that determines membership in a Native nation, but rather one's citizenship status. As such, the argument that tribal governments are racially exclusive is false.

Despite being incorrect, alleging that tribal courts are *racially* exclusive serves multiple purposes in the argument against VAWA 2013. On one level it delegitimizes tribal national governments by constructing them as simply the governing bodies of race-based cultural organizations. On another level, it appeals to one of the most accessible values in the modern American zeitgeist: racial equality. Despite being a country that was forged from the original sins of African enslavement and American Indian genocide, the United States prides itself on the progress that it has made towards a society in which race no longer matters. The hard-won gains in racial equality that are codified in the U.S. Constitution are often cited as both a source of pride, as well as evidence that we now live in a post-racial society. Unfortunately, the existence of "racially exclusive" courts and governments challenge that, thereby undermining a colorblind ideal. Arguments like Grassley's and the Heritage Foundation's exploit pre-existing anxiety over racial inequality to obfuscate the issue of tribal sovereignty. Contending that investing in tribal sovereignty is the true source of racism in this debate conveniently sidesteps very real problems of racialized gender violence against Native women.

By shifting the focus away from *real* racialized violence and instead towards the *perceived* racism of tribal governments, oppositional discourse ironically implicates Native nations as the true perpetrators of racism in Indian country. While this may appear absurd in a debate over solving violence against Native women, flipping the script in this way is congruent with the narrative developed in this research. Here, jurisdictional conflicts have arisen from law and policy attempting to solve the "Indian problem" by, among other things, addressing white anxiety over "savage" Native justice. By centering the white experience of *perceived* violence in Indian country, the federal government has consistently contributed to *real* experiences of violence in Indian country.

As noted in Chapter Three, when jurisdiction was restored to the Lakota Nation after Crow Dog (Kȟaŋǧí Šúŋka) killed Spotted Tail (Siŋté Gleškáá), Native justice was read as the absence of justice. Due to white anxiety over the perceived incompetency of Native governments in Crow Dog's case, Congress passed the Major Crimes Act of 1885—one of the first of many laws that created jurisdictional conflicts in Indian country today. In Chapter Three, I illustrated that undergirding the laws responsible for jurisdictional conflicts in the prosecution of sexual violence against Native women is the pervasive myth of Native savagery. The Major Crimes Act (1885), Public Law 280 (1953), and *Oliphant v. Suquamish* (1978) all relied on racist assumptions that Native people were not competent to manage crime and punishment, and that to allow Native nations to exercise jurisdiction as part of their inherent sovereignty would not only spurn the civilization process, but would also threaten white safety. To illustrate this, I noted that the 1978 Oliphant decision was justified through 1891 case law, which held that Congress should regulate Indian jurisdiction in a manner "thought to be consistent with the safety of the white population in which they may have come in contact."[29]

Those who oppose Title IX of VAWA 2013 by propagating the same discourse responsible for the laws that have created jurisdictional conflicts, continue to invoke the fear of Native savagery to deliver an anti-sovereignty argument. In doing so, they communicate the message that the *perceived* threat of legal violence against non-Native (read: white) Americans is more important than the *real* experience of sexual violence against Native women. In that way, Grassley and others engage a paradigm of rape culture to invest in American hegemony by further marginalizing Native people. Rape culture naturalizes sexual violence as normal[30] and values the experience of the perpetrator over the experience of the victim. Anti-Title IX sentiment overwhelmingly focuses on its (unfounded) potential for violating the rights of the accused, rather than focus on the rights of the survivor and her community. This is evidenced by the fact that many people in Congress would rather allow the VAWA as a whole to expire (affecting millions of American women both Native and non-Native), rather than allow this modest expansion of tribal jurisdiction. Indian affairs lawyer Ryan Dreveskracht challenged this conservative reframing of violence with the following statement noted in the epigraph of this chapter:

> Unfortunately, certain Republicans are singing the old song of "unsophisticated tribal courts and uneducated tribal judges" to stop the bill from going forward [...] I say, if you don't trust the ability of tribal courts to be fair and just, don't go to the reservation and rape women—but that's just my take.[31]

Here, Dreveskracht rightly places blame for sexual assault on the perpetrator who chooses to commit sexual violence in Indian country, rather than focus on the perceived incompetence of Native nations to adjudicate crime. In doing so he indicts misguided notions of "justice" in the anti-Title IX argument and calls out the rape culture that bolsters it.

In Title IX discourse, opponents invoke the logic of rape culture to reject anti-colonial solutions to a deeply colonial problem. This is unsurprising since, as Chapter Four illustrated, sexual violence against Native women has always been enmeshed with colonial law and policy. Examining anti-Title IX arguments illustrates that the same damaging assumptions undergirding the federal Indian policy of the past continue to challenge the Native anti-violence/pro-sovereignty movement today. However, unlike Congressional testimony debating the Major Crimes Act and other laws that led to jurisdictional conflicts, anti-Title IX arguments were ultimately unsuccessful. This begs the questions: does the passage of a VAWA with an intact Title IX signify a sea change in federal policy towards Native people? What does this mean for Native women, the anti-violence movement and the future of Native sovereignty vis-à-vis the U.S.? By examining the mechanics of

Title IX, its promises, its limitations, and how it is perceived by Native women and their communities, we can assess its potential as an anti-violence strategy and discuss what work may still need to be done.

Title IX: Policy, Perception and Potential

By 2013, Deborah Parker, vice-chair of the Tulalip Tribes, had already spent three years flying back and forth between Washington State and Washington, D.C., lobbying Congress to strengthen federal protections for Native women.[32] Like many Native women, Parker understood first hand the way that jurisdictional conflicts maintain and inscribe violence in Indian country, stating that when she grew up:

> We didn't have a strong police presence when I was younger. Even [if you called] the police, often they didn't respond [...] When they did, they would say, "Oh, it's not our jurisdiction, sorry." [And] prosecutors wouldn't show up.[33]

With personal experience to strengthen her resolve, Parker pushed back against solutions to violence against Native women that merely increased federal and state power in Indian country. Instead, in the time since the passage of the Tribal Law and Order Act of 2010 (TLOA), Parker has fought for solutions that invest in tribal sovereignty. Parker, as part of a broad coalition of Native advocates, engaged the hard-won battle that resulted in Title IX of VAWA 2013. Unlike the TLOA, which prescribes more federal/state intervention into tribal justice systems, Title IX imagines the possibility of Native governments as the arbiters of justice in their own communities.

As noted, Title IX offers special domestic violence criminal jurisdiction to federally recognized tribes over some crimes committed by some non-Native perpetrators in Indian country. In breaking with the tradition of limiting Native sovereignty, Parker and others argue that Title IX is the most significant investment in tribal sovereignty by the federal government in recent history.[34] Parker places Title IX in a historic context by stating, "there hasn't been major tribal legislation that grants inherent tribal authority since the historic days of treaty times [...] this will have a substantial impact on our sovereign ability to govern."[35]

Parker's support of these hard-won provisions is indicative of the larger sentiment expressed in the Native community where Title IX is seen as a decolonizing event that is a victory for all tribes. As Colville writer Dina Gilio-Whitaker notes:

> [Title IX of VAWA 2013] was a huge victory for Indian country not only because it addresses one of the biggest problems in Native communities (gender-based violence),

> but also because the Major Crimes Act is one of the primary impediments to true tribal self-government. VAWA thus indicates a strengthening of self-determination.[36]

The chair of the Board of Trustees of the Confederated Tribes of the Umatilla Indian Reservation (CTUIR), Gary Burke, adds, "This is important not only for the CTUIR in exercising and expanding our sovereignty, but for the sovereignty of all tribes."[37]

Parker, Gilio-Whitaker, and Burke's statements give insight into the way that Title IX is empowering to Native women and nations. Here, the law is perceived not only as something that can address violence against Native women specifically, but also as a tool that can help decolonize broadly. As a decolonial tool, Title IX is potentially transformative in that it addresses violence by strengthening tribal sovereignty. As Gilio-Whitaker's statement indicates, Title IX shifts the focus of mainstream anti-violence legislation to address gender violence as part of a colonial (rather than individual) pathology.

Title IX is indeed a sea change in federal Indian policy, which reflects resistance by Native women and communities to American oppression. Despite that, there is evidence to suggest that while VAWA 2013 is promising in its anti-violence potential, it is also quite problematic in the way that it frames solutions vis-à-vis the U.S. federal government. My research acknowledges the agency of the Native women and communities whose work resulted in the creation of Title IX and the passage of VAWA 2013. This effort is inline with the transformative work that Native communities have always done to challenge American colonialism. With deference to those whose work facilitated this watershed moment in Native sovereignty, there are many aspects of VAWA 2013 and Title IX that warrant critique. While Title IX is indeed a landmark, there are many ways in which it furthers a colonial narrative that has always invested in American legal hegemony. The following section identifies the shortcomings of VAWA 2013 not to minimize its potential, but rather to critique its limitations in an effort to benefit the Native anti-violence movement.

Whose Lives Matter? Domestic Violence and the Construction of the "Other" in VAWA 2013

Title IX of VAWA 2013 addresses violence against Native women in Indian country by extending "special domestic violence jurisdiction" to "participating tribes" for some crimes perpetrated by non-Native offenders in Indian country. As noted in Chapter Three, criminal jurisdiction in Indian country is predicated on both the location of the crime and the racial identity of the perpetrator and victim. Title IX adds to this by using the type of crime (domestic/non-domestic) and the relationship between the perpetrator and the community as determinants as well. Title IX extends criminal jurisdiction to tribal governments over non-Native perpetrators in cases of "dating violence," "domestic violence," and violations of protection orders. Title IX applies to perpetrators who "reside in the Indian country of the participating tribe," are "employed in the Indian country of the participating tribe," or are a "spouse, intimate partner, or dating partner" of a Native person in Indian country.[38]

Considering that 86% of violence against Native women is perpetrated by non-Native men, extending tribal jurisdiction to include interracial assault is significant. Unlike the Tribal Law and Order Act, Title IX of VAWA 2013 begins to vest tribes with the power to address the perpetrators of the vast majority of sexual assault against Native women. Therefore any provisions that extend tribal jurisdiction over non-Native perpetrators can be read as major step forward for tribal governments to more fully govern the people within their nations.

Despite the potential of Title IX, it falls short both in its limited application as well as its theoretical approach. While the provisions in Title IX have the potential to address *some* of the violence that Native women experience in Indian country, it is quite narrow in scope. Title IX does not include sexual violence perpetrated by people without significant ties to the community, violence committed against Native women that is not domestic in nature, and (unless it is in violation of a protection order) Title IX does not cover child abuse or elder abuse.[39] Considering that the U.S. Department of Justice's own reports reveal that strangers perpetrate the majority of sexual assault against Native women, using pre-existing relationship status to determine jurisdiction is significantly limiting.[40] Additionally, Title IX does nothing to address jurisdictional complications stemming from land division under the Dawes Act and nothing to address the problem of competing jurisdictional authority of state and federal governments. Finally, when the bill was signed into law, Title IX specifically excluded Alaska Native nations from exercising special domestic violence jurisdiction—meaning that under no circumstances could an Alaska Native government adjudicate a crime perpetrated by a non-Native offender.[41, 42]

Since tribes may not exercise jurisdiction over non-Native defendants who have no established tie to the community, Title IX does nothing to address predatory violence perpetrated by non-Native people who seek out Indian country because of jurisdictional impunity. And, while Title IX is celebrated for challenging the Oliphant decision, it ironically does not cover the type of crime that created *Oliphant v. Suquamish*. As a resident of the Port Madison Indian Reservation, Mark David Oliphant had significant ties to the community. Yet, because he assaulted a tribal police officer and not a domestic partner, Title IX would not apply in his case. Unfortunately, should another *Oliphant* present itself, tribes will still be powerless to prosecute it.

Considering the variety of sexual violence that Native women experience in Indian country, including sexual violence that is not domestic, jurisdiction over non-Native perpetrators under Title IX is significantly limited.[43] In a law that attempts to address violence against all women in general—with provisions that attempt to provide "Safety for Indian Women" in particular—one questions the value of including relationship-based restrictions in Title IX of VAWA 2013. In theorizing this law as a break from traditional colonial narratives, and a potential tool in anti-violence strategies, we must ask ourselves: Why are tribal governments seen as legitimate authorities to adjudicate crime on their land only in "special" cases? Whose experience of violence matters and under what circumstances?

To answer these questions, one could argue that extending tribal jurisdiction over non-Native perpetrators who have ties to the community is a logical first step. As noted in Chapter Three, law enforcement is most effective when it is local and directly accountable to those it serves. And, considering the fact that the Dawes Act created a large non-Native community in Indian country, it would make sense to start with non-Native residents when expanding tribal jurisdiction. But if VAWA 2013 is willing to acknowledge the importance of local control over one's community, then by that logic shouldn't *anyone* who commits a crime in Indian country be held accountable to the tribe? Since Congress has specifically decided to limit this accountability, it begs the question: What purpose could these limitations serve for the federal government that created them?

In the *Harvard Law Review*'s "Congress Recognizes and Affirms Tribal Courts' Special Domestic Violence Jurisdiction Over Non-Indian Defendants," the authors address these questions, arguing that extending and limiting tribal jurisdiction serves a number of purposes for the federal government. On one level, it is a strategic move that re-establishes Congress's dominance over the judicial branch. By extending jurisdiction over non-Native perpetrators, Congress challenges *Oliphant*. Yet, by precluding a jurisdictional challenge to a scenario similar to *Oliphant*, Congress also ensures that the judicial branch won't rule Title IX unconstitutional should it be challenged in court. Congress does this, the authors argue, because it acknowledges "the Court's discomfort with the perceived democratic illegitimacy of tribal governments,"[44] and therefore strategically pre-emptively limits tribal jurisdiction to maintain the integrity of Title IX as a whole.

Placating the "perceived democratic illegitimacy of tribal governments" by limiting tribal sovereignty, rather than challenging those perceptions themselves, is an enduring legacy of federal Indian policy. The *Harvard Law Review* authors continue to illustrate this through their attention to the relationship clauses of

Title IX. They argue that by creating a law that only covers non-Native defendants with significant ties to the community, Congress "responds directly to the concern that tribal court criminal jurisdiction over nonmembers offends the liberal ideal of a government legitimized by the consent of the governed."[45] In other words, individuals who voluntarily enter into a relationship with Indian country through residency, employment, or intimate relationship, imply their consent to tribal accountability. By excluding those who enter Indian country without establishing those ties, Congress addresses the "*any* American" fear articulated by Senator Hutchison. Though this may be read as a shrewd political move by the legislature, it nevertheless shows a continued commitment to structuring law based on the *perceived* fear of Native justice systems, rather than on the *real* experiences of Native people. The authors argue that doing so continues the legacy of delivering Native people out of savagery and into civilization by imposing a "significant overlay of 'American values'" over Native justice systems.[46] Therefore, limiting the scope of Title IX is really about furthering the civilizing project of Native people by inscribing liberal cultural values through their governing bodies. Ultimately, the authors argue that the jurisdictional limitation in Title IX, "is primarily a statement about values—the value of tribal sovereignty, the value of liberal ideals, the proper balance between them, and above all, Congress's role in fixing that balance."[47] Again, the ghost of Kȟaŋǧí Šúŋka seems to be making an appearance, as the same discourse that undergirded the Major Crimes Act of 1885 continues to make its way into federal Indian policy today.

These nineteenth-century attitudes about Native justice were present in the 2013 conflict between pro-sovereignty activists and those who still cling to the notion that tribal justice is ineffectual, unfair and dangerous. This is exemplified by the exclusion of Alaska Native nations in the final version of VAWA 2013. As *Indian Country Today Media Network* reported, Title IX's original language did not exclude Alaska Native communities but was likely changed as a compromise to ensure its passage in both houses of Congress due to legislators who "feared advancing Native jurisdiction in the 'last frontier' state."[48] It is interesting to note that the only state specifically excluded from Title IX protections under VAWA 2013 is also known as the "last frontier." This highlights the perception of Alaska as the last true border between a wholly domesticated America and a pre-contact wilderness. And significantly, it is within this "wild" space that the notion of Native people as unable to administer justice continued. Here, excluding Alaska Native nations under Title IX reemphasized the colonial narrative that Native justice is antithetical to the project of furthering American civilization. Significantly, the VAWA was amended in December 2014 to re-incorporate Alaska Native nations into the special domestic violence jurisdiction provisions.[49] While this is a positive step for tribal sovereignty, the fact that it was necessary to exclude 40% of Native nations in order placate those who opposed modest changes to jurisdiction in Indian country speaks to the magnitude of the anti-tribal sovereignty sentiment in the federal government.

As Native demographics are ranked in order to address non-Native pushback against Native sovereignty, the fear of Native justice continues to have very real outcomes for Native women and their communities. In VAWA 2013, Title IX appears to rely on familiar racist assumptions about tribal governments in order to make judgments about who is more deserving of both political and corporal sovereignty. In this case, the sovereignty of Native nations in the continental United States was privileged over those in Alaska, and other restrictions based on the type of crime (domestic/non-domestic) and perpetrator/community relationship appear to make value judgments of whose experience of violence warrants local (and therefore more effective) attention. Since extending tribal jurisdiction promises to address the root cause of jurisdictional conflicts and the sexual violence they invite, then limiting the *political* sovereignty of Native nations under VAWA 2013 limits the *corporal* sovereignty of Native women in Indian country. Those who are excluded are thus devalued under Title IX.

Unfortunately, creating hierarchies that value the experiences of some women over others has characterized the VAWA since its inception. As legal scholar Kimberlé Crenshaw argued in "Mapping the Margins: Intersectionality, Identity Politics, and Violence Against Women of Color," women of color have consistently been marginalized in the VAWA because the overwhelmingly white male legislature could only understand violence against women as a whole from the perspective of violence against white women in particular. Here, the range of violence experienced by women of color was not recognized, and as such solutions under the VAWA replicated pre-existing racial hierarchies.[50] Understanding this history helps us to theorize how some Native women are included (and thus valued) while others are excluded. While domestic violence may be an experience that is relatable to the mainstream anti-violence movement (and therefore centered in Title IX), the predatory violence of non-Native strangers who exploit Indian country jurisdiction to prey on Native women is unique to the Native community and is therefore ultimately excluded.

Institutionalizing hierarchies based on non-normative experiences of violence is apparent in much of the anti-VAWA 2013 discourse. For opponents, the provisions that protect Native women through enhanced tribal jurisdiction were often part of an aversion toward protecting marginalized communities in general. In addition to extending jurisdiction for Native communities, VAWA 2013 also proposed enhanced protections for immigrant women and members of the

LGBT community. As such, the pushback against Native sovereignty was often coupled with anti-immigrant, anti-LGBT sentiment.[51] For example, in an interview on MSNBC, U.S. Representative Marsha Blackburn (R-TN) expressed her opposition to VAWA 2013 in the context of not wanting to include these new demographics. When asked why she wasn't supporting the reauthorization of the VAWA, she replied:

> What you do is you begin to dilute the money that needs to go into these sexual assault centers [...] When you start to make [the VAWA] about other things and it becomes an "against violence act" and not a targeted focused act that is there to address the issue of violence against women [...] I didn't like the way it was expanded to include *other different groups*. What you need is something that is focused specifically to help these shelters and to help *our* law enforcement [emphasis mine].[52]

In this statement, Blackburn constructs the "Other" in Native women, immigrant women, and members of the LGBT community. Existing in opposition to those deserving of VAWA resources, Blackburn frames creating additional legal protections for "other different groups" as draining resources from "our" institutions. While "our" institutions like shelters and mainstream law enforcement are not exclusive of Native women, immigrant women and the LBGT community, she discusses their importance in terms of a value-based hierarchy. Women who utilize mainstream anti-violence resources are seen as more worthy of services than "other different groups" who may need different resources (such as increased local control and political sovereignty) to address the unique experiences of violence in their communities.

In response to Blackburn and others, Representative Gwen Moore (D-WI) gave an impassioned speech on the House floor of Congress. Discussing the House version of the VAWA that removed protections for Native women, immigrant women, and members of the LGBT community, Moore challenged the "Otherizing" of marginalized women:

> I pray that [the House] will do as the Senate has done and come together as one to protect ALL women from violence. As I think about the LGBT victims that are not [in the House bill], the Native women who are not [in the House bill], the immigrants who are not included in [the House bill], I would say, as Sojourner Truth would say, AIN'T THEY WOMEN?! They deserve protections. We talk about the constitutional right... Don't women on tribal lands deserve the constitutional right of equal protection and not to be raped and battered and beaten and dragged back onto Native lands because they know they can be raped with impunity? AIN'T THEY WOMEN?! [emphasis in original][53]

Moore's speech notes the way that Blackburn's argument against "other different groups" draining "our" resources, fits within a larger history of creating the "Other" in gender-based movements. In her speech, Moore invoked the legacy of Sojourner Truth, a nineteenth-century activist who indicted the mainstream women's rights movement for claiming to be a movement for "all women," while actively excluding the experiences of African American women like herself. At the Women's Convention of 1851, Truth challenged her audience, asking, "Ain't I a woman?"—meaning shouldn't a movement that is ostensibly about the rights of "all women" acknowledge the way that Black women's lives differ from their white counterparts?

Noting a tradition of excluding marginalized groups and creating demographic hierarchies, Moore engages Truth's legacy to hold the VAWA accountable to its own goal of addressing violence against *all* women. Here, not only does Moore situate her support of an intact VAWA 2013 in this historical context, but she also engages with Native sovereignty and jurisdiction as part of her argument. By illustrating how perpetrators prey on Native women in Indian country by manipulating jurisdiction, Moore delivers a strong message that the goal of addressing violence against all women under the VAWA cannot be realized without attention to tribal sovereignty.

The advocacy of Moore and other intersectional feminists led the House to pass a version of the VAWA that included protection for these "other" women. Today, provisions for Native women, immigrant women and members of the LGBT community are the law of the land under VAWA 2013.[54] Passing an intact VAWA 2013 is important in that new provisions for marginalized groups challenge the history of "Othering" women in the anti-violence movement. However, while I give deference to Moore for fighting for provisions for Native women, the outcome of her activism is not beyond critique. As the next section will explore, Moore's argument for Title IX—while liberal—is certainly not radical. Instead, it continues to invest in American hegemony while domesticating tribal jurisdiction. By problematizing liberal solutions in the context of radical feminism, we can continue to theorize the most effective solutions to jurisdictional conflicts and sexual violence against Native women in Indian country.

"Safety for Indian Women" as Assimilation for Tribal Governments? Reexamining the Paradigm of "Law and Order"

Despite being a point of departure from previous versions of the VAWA, VAWA 2013 is still limited on both practical and theoretical levels. In practice, Title IX only addresses *some* types of violence against *some* Native women, thereby continuing to inscribe value-laden hierarchies onto Native women's experiences of violence. Additionally, as this section will show, Title IX is also limited on a theoretical level because it is still structured by a colonial impulse to address problems of "law and order" in Indian country through assimilating tribal governments.

In her 2012 dissertation, *Un-Settling Questions: The Construction of Indigeneity and Violence Against Native Women*, Kimberly Robertson invoked the title of the 2010 Tribal Law and Order Act (TLOA) to problematize the paradigm of "law and order" as an organizing principle under American hegemony. Referencing Luana Ross's *Inventing the Savage: The Social Construction of Native American Criminality*, Robertson notes that the paradigm of "law and order" has itself been used to disappear Native people under American colonialism.[55] In *Inventing the Savage*, Ross illustrates how historically Native identity itself was made illegal through criminalizing Native culture (like religious practices). This bolstered the carceral state, thereby disappearing Native people into the criminal justice system. At the same time, as a response to the perceived savagery of Native justice systems, establishing "law and order" in Native communities has traditionally taken the form of colonizing Native justice systems. As I demonstrated in Chapter Five, the TLOA is yet another example of this, in which "law and order" is achieved through colonizing tribal justice while increasing the policing and incarceration of Native men.

Robertson's reading of "law and order," helps to further theorize the significance of VAWA 2013. Though VAWA 2013 breaks from the TLOA in that it does extend some limited jurisdiction over non-Native perpetrators, it continues to employ an assimilative "law and order" approach that assumes American legal supremacy while investing in the prison-industrial complex. It is these twin paradigms of assimilation and incarceration under the banner of "law and order" that form the foundation of my final critique of Title IX.

The first section of this chapter spends a significant amount of time debunking the argument that Title IX is unconstitutional. While it is important to challenge these false allegations and theorize why the trope of "unconstitutionality" becomes a handy tool to dismantle Native sovereignty, it is also important to question the relevance of constitutionality in a debate over tribal jurisdiction. As noted, Native nations are both pre- and extra-constitutional entities, possessing an inherent sovereignty that was affirmed by the U.S. Constitution and the treaty-making process. Despite that, Congress has consistently seen fit to domesticate Native sovereignty and vest itself with plenary power over Native nations.[56] Liberal solutions to jurisdictional conflicts and sexual violence against Native women (while distinct from the racist assumptions that undergird anti-Title IX discourse) still normalize the federal government as the natural custodian of tribal sovereignty.

Rather than take a radical decolonial approach centered on the inherent sovereignty of Native nations, pro-Title IX arguments often fall into the liberal trope of "liberating" Native nations from federal control by assimilating their governments into Western legal hegemony. Arguing whether jurisdictional extensions under Title IX are constitutional naturalizes the notion that tribal sovereignty is something that should be controlled by the federal government, rather than something that exists outside of it. While Gwen Moore's powerful speech is important, it still places the value of Native women within colonial power structures. Here, Native women deserve justice because they are *American*, not because they are members of sovereign entities whose experience of violence is created and maintained by *America*. By framing Native women's rights as valid because of the "constitutional right of equal protection," Moore places tribal sovereignty as something that is, and should be, within the purview of the federal government.

Other liberal proponents of extending tribal sovereignty under Title IX fall into a similar trap. For example, Troy Eid, attorney and chair of the Indian Law and Order Commission, argued against jurisdictional restrictions in *Oliphant* by arguing for "extending tribal court jurisdiction to all citizens in a way that fully protects their rights under the U.S. Constitution."[57] He later supported tribal jurisdictional extensions under Title IX when tribal governments "agree voluntarily to integrate federal constitutional substantive and procedural protections into their justice systems."[58] As Robertson points out in *Unsettling Questions*, Eid's arguments are on par with the overall paternalism in federal Indian policy that grants rights to Native nations only when they are willing to participate in the colonization of their own governments. This is very much in line with the paradigm of "law and order" in the TLOA, where federal Indian policy only invests in tribal justice systems from an assimilationist approach. Robertson notes that while the attempt at civilizing Native justice systems can be framed as empowering Native nations, it ultimately comes from a desire to "do away with Native identity altogether so that Native peoples can be incorporated into a more homogenous and, thus, more manageable US citizenry."[59] This colonial impulse is present in the final versions of the TLOA and VAWA 2013 where both laws extend rights to Native nations only when they operate within the paradigm of American legal hegemony.

With this in mind, I challenge liberal arguments that situate Native justice systems within the American mainstream, and instead advance a more radical framing of justice, jurisdiction and anti-violence activism. While liberal solutions are necessary to challenge the racism of anti-sovereignty discourse, they unfortunately reify the federal government's legal hegemony over Native nations. For example, liberal arguments for enhanced tribal jurisdiction posit that extended rights should be granted to tribal courts because these courts are up to the standard of the American justice systems (or have the potential to be with federal support). They also tend to see the federal government as the most appropriate entity to address jurisdictional conflicts and sexual violence against Native women by either increasing federal power in Indian country, or by teaching Native governments how to properly adjudicate crimes. These arguments ignore the inherent sovereignty of Native nations while also refusing to acknowledge the federal government itself as the most significant perpetrator of violence against Native women and nations. As such I advocate for a radical re-reading of Title IX as something that can play a *role* in addressing violence against Native women, but as something that—left unchecked—can actually further inscribe colonial violence in Native communities.

Native legal scholar Sarah Deer notes the problems with liberal solutions in her discussion of VAWA 2013. While I illustrated in Chapter Five how "law and order" for Native nations under the TLOA specifically meant incorporation into American legal hegemony, Deer extends this analysis to VAWA 2013:

> [A]nd when tribal governments receive VAWA funding, they feel compelled to replicate the state or federal justice system. I've seen situations where tribes have been discouraged from reinvigorating a traditional response to violence that would involve the community and the women themselves rather than the tribal court. But the state systems and federal systems have never worked to protect Native women—they've always worked to penalize Native women for being Native. When tribes replicate that model, the solutions to violence become very difficult to find.[60]

Deer's argument illustrates that VAWA 2013 continues to encourage assimilation *into* American legal hegemony without addressing the violence *caused by* American legal hegemony. Thus, liberal solutions can do little to dismantle the colonial context in which violence against Native women occurs.

Theorizing Solutions: Radicalizing VAWA 2013

Perhaps the *Harvard Law Review* put it best when they referred to special domestic violence jurisdiction under VAWA 2013 as a "cautious experiment, not a revolution."[61] While it may be tempting to view Title IX as the final solution to jurisdictional conflicts and the sexual violence they facilitate in Indian country, like the TLOA, it is limited in its capacity to accomplish this. While VAWA 2013 is a watershed moment that takes its point of departure from the TLOA to challenge

Oliphant by investing in tribal sovereignty, it falls within a paradigm still deeply entrenched in maintaining American hegemony over Native people.

Ultimately, VAWA 2013 is a liberal solution for a radical problem, which frames change as a moral imperative rather than a sovereign right. Even though liberal ideology eventually defeated oppositional discourse, VAWA 2013 is still rooted in an effort by the United States to "help" "other" women, rather than recognizing that those women already possess the power to help themselves through the inherent sovereignty of their nations. Because jurisdictional conflicts are rooted in the colonial violence that has leveraged both legal and sexual violence to disenfranchise Native people, anti-violence strategies in Indian country must employ decolonial solutions and cannot come solely from the federal government.

Liberal arguments for federal solutions to jurisdictional conflicts and sexual violence against Native women are fundamentally flawed because they invest in an assimilationist paradigm that doesn't break with the colonial assumption of Native savagery. However, radical solutions that preclude *any* use of federal policy to address violence in Indian country are themselves deeply marginalizing. While it is important to problematize Title IX, completely dismissing it would be a mistake. Precluding Title IX as relevant in the anti-violence movement disregards Native women like Deborah Parker who fought for enhanced tribal jurisdiction in the wake of the TLOA, and women of color like Gwen Moore who resisted the "Otherizing" of subaltern women in the VAWA. Instead, like the TLOA, I argue for the incorporation of Title IX as part of the solution to violence in Indian country, within a larger decolonial anti-violence movement.

This multifaceted approach is part of the way that Native women and Native governments conceptualize VAWA 2013 today. As stated in *Indian Country Today*, while the TLOA and VAWA 2013 "do not give the tribes criminal jurisdiction over non-Indians except in the domestic violence context, and thus are insufficient," they do "provide tribal governments an opportunity to lay the foundation for the broader reform [...]."[62] Here, while VAWA 2013 is not seen as *the* solution, it is seen as *part of* the solution—one that represents a "foundation" despite being "insufficient."

The Pascua Yaqui tribe, the first Native nation to exercise special domestic violence jurisdiction over a non-Native perpetrator,[63] expressed a similar sentiment in a press release:

> While we still may have many problems and this is certainly only a first step, the fact that we have implemented VAWA 2013 is momentous. When we reflect on the historical words and actions of our elders, especially those who have passed on, we are blessed to have the opportunity to do as they did: protect our people.[64]

By engaging with VAWA 2013 as a "first step," the Pascua Yaqui situate enhanced jurisdiction under Title IX in the tradition of engaging with a variety of strategies to protect their people as they have always done. In an article penned in 2012 during the controversy over reauthorizing the VAWA, Sarah Deer echoed the Pascua Yaqui's tradition noting, "there is no greater exercise of sovereignty than protecting our own people."[65] Therefore exercising jurisdiction under Title IX, while limited, is still a genuine expression of the inherent sovereignty that has always characterized Native nations.

In her article "Violence Against Women and Tribal Law," Deer discussed how expanded jurisdictional authority, as part of a reauthorized VAWA, is a tool that can be leveraged to help Native nations address violence in their own communities. However, given the limitations of Title IX, Deer offers radical solutions that exist outside of VAWA 2013. While supporting Title IX and advocating for reform in federal Indian policy, she also encourages tribal governments to forge solutions that exist outside of the federal government. Some of these solutions include: encouraging tribal governments to develop and implement their own tribal justice codes independent of the federal government; instituting procedures to make sure tribes don't employ people with violent criminal records; decolonizing existing tribal justice codes modeled after American jurisprudence; indigenizing tribal law to engage with traditional notions of justice; and circumventing federal law to prosecute crime.[66] Central to Deer's argument is employing a differential consciousness to work both *within* and *outside* of existing power structures in order to address jurisdictional conflicts and violence in Indian country. While Deer is an advocate for enhanced jurisdiction in the reauthorization of the VAWA, her advocacy is tempered by decolonial solutions which themselves aren't predicated on action by the federal government.

Deer's vision of tribal justice engages with Mohawk scholar Taiaiake Alfred's notion of the true meaning of sovereignty. In his chapter in *Sovereignty Matters*, Alfred argues that sovereignty isn't *given,* it is *inherent.*[67] While the federal government at first recognized Native sovereignty, and then later encroached upon it, Alfred argues that it didn't just disappear. In other words, just because the federal government makes laws that limit tribal sovereignty, doesn't mean that it extinguishes the sovereignty intrinsic to a pre-constitutional entity. Because sovereignty is *inherent,* the federal government ultimately is powerless to limit or extinguish it. Framing anti-violence strategies from Alfred's perspective can be part of forging radical solutions for a radical problem. Rather than focus on ways Native activists can pressure the U.S. government to restore tribal sovereignty, a radical perspective challenges the notion that the federal government has the power to give or take away sovereignty at all. As Deer notes, "tribal governments must be ready to take action on our own terms when women are assaulted," and rather than waiting for the federal government to create a solution, "we can start now."[68] It is from this vantage that Native women and communities can leverage both VAWA 2013 *and* independent decolonial strategies in order to comprehensively address jurisdictional conflicts and sexual violence against Native women.

Notes

1. As quoted in Rob Capriccioso, "Tribal Provisions of Women Safety Law Under Senate Attack." *Indian Country Today Media Network*. Web. 01 Apr. 2012. <http://indiancountrytodaymedianetwork.com/2012/04/01/tribal-provisions-women-safety-law-under-senate-attack-105634> Accessed 01 Oct. 2014.
2. "Sen. Grassley Doesn't Think Native Americans Can Hold Fair Trials." YouTube. *Think Progress*. Web. 20 Feb. 2013. <https://www.youtube.com/watch?v=BRpjxtLrTcE> Accessed 19 Oct. 2014.
3. Note—in previous House and Senate versions of the bill, the provisions that became Title IX may have appeared in sections that differ from the final law. Since the language of these provisions is essentially the same, I categorize opposition to special domestic violence jurisdiction in Indian country as opposition to Title IX unless otherwise noted.
4. S. 47—113th Congress: Violence Against Women Reauthorization Act of 2013.
5. Ibid.
6. This includes Sen. Ted Cruz (R-TX), Sen. Jim Risch (R-ID), Sen. Rand Paul (R-KT), and Sen. Mike Lee (R-UT).
7. David B. Mulhausen and Christina Villegas, "Violence Against Women Act: Reauthorization Fundamentally Flawed." *Heritage Foundation*. Web. 29 Mar. 2012. <http://www.heritage.org/research/reports/2012/03/the-violence-against-women-act-reauthorization-fundamentally-flawed> Accessed 19 Oct. 2014.
8. Ibid.
9. Quoted from Sen. Ron Johnson (R-WI) in Craig Gilbert, "Sen. Ron Johnson Calls Violence Against Women Bill Unconstitutional" *Journal Sentinel*. Web. 13 Feb. 2013. <http://www.jsonline.com/blogs/news/191035431.html> Accessed 19 Oct. 2014.
10. Family Research Council, "Form letter: Vote 'No' on S. 47," 1 Feb. 2013.
11. See for example Ryan Dreveskracht's discussion of *U.S. v. Lara* (2004) in Rob Capriccioso, "House Republican VAWA Bill Offers Strong Tribal Protections; Will Cantor Accept?" *Indian Country Today Media Network*. Web. 22 Feb. 2013. <http://indiancountrytodaymedianetwork.com/2013/02/22/house-republican-vawa-bill-offers-strong-tribal-protections-will-cantor-accept-147851> Accessed 19 Oct. 2014.
12. Steven Pevar, *The Rights of Indians and Tribes: The Authoritative ACLU Guide to Indian Tribal Rights* (Carbondale: Southern Illinois University Press, 1992).
13. M. Brent Leonhard, "Closing a Gap in Indian Country Justice: Oliphant, Lara and DOJ's Proposed Fix." *Harvard Law Journal On Racial & Ethnic Justice* 28 (2012): 117–71.
14. Note that even in treaties that did not expressly grant criminal jurisdiction, treaties are not a grant of rights *to* Native people, but rather a grant of rights *from* Native people. Therefore,

unless specifically extinguished in a treaty, it is assumed that Native nations maintain the sovereign right of criminal jurisdiction. See Pevar, *The Rights of Indians and Tribes*, 2012.

15. Alexandria Baca, "Sen. John Cornyn Cites Tribal Provision in Vote Against Anti-violence Bill." *Dallas News*. Web. 13 Feb. 2013. <http://trailblazersblog.dallasnews.com/2013/02/sen-cornyn-votes-against-anti-violence-bill-cites-unconstitutional-amendment.html/> Accessed 01 Oct. 2014.
16. Pete Kasperowicz, "House Passes Violence Against Women Act Reauthorization." *The Hill*. Web. 16 May 2012. <http://thehill.com/blogs/floor-action/house/227877-house-passes-violence-against-women-act-reauthorization> Accessed 01 Oct. 2014.
17. "'No' on the Violence Against Women Act (VAWA)," *Heritage Action for America, Senate Key Votes*. Web. 04 Feb. 2013. <http://heritageaction.com/key-votes/no-on-the-violence-against-women-act-vawa/> Accessed 01 Oct. 2014.
18. National Center on Domestic and Sexual Violence. "The Safeguards in the Violence Against Women Act (VAWA)." Web. 2011. <http://www.ncdsv.org/images/NatlTFEndSDVAW_Safeguards%20in%20VAWA_2011.pdf> Accessed 01 Oct. 2014.
19. Maria Cantwell, "In Floor Speech, Cantwell Urges Swift Passage of Violence Against Women Act with Strong Tribal Provisions." Maria Cantwell, United States Senator for Washington. Web. 7 Feb. 2013. <http://www.cantwell.senate.gov/public/index.cfm/2013/2/in-floor-speech-cantwell-urges-swift-passage-of-violence-against-women-act-with-strong-tribal-provisions> Accessed 01 Oct. 2014.
20. For example the TLOA imposed sentencing limitations of no more than three years imprisonment and a $15,000 for each offense adjudicated in tribal court (see Chapter Five).
21. National Center on Domestic and Sexual Violence: National Task Force to End Sexual Domestic Violence Against Women, "Heritage Action is Wrong About its VAWA Claims." Web 2013. <http://www.ncdsv.org/images/NatlTFEndSDVAW_Safeguards%20in%20VAWA_2011.pdf> Accessed 01 Oct. 2014.
22. S. 47—113th Congress: Violence Against Women Reauthorization Act of 2013.
23. Ibid.
24. See text of the U.S. Constitution, Article 6 and Scott Keyes, "Top GOP Senator: Native American Juries Are Incapable Of Trying White People Fairly." *ThinkProgress*. Web. 21 Feb. 2013. <http://thinkprogress.org/justice/2013/02/21/1619501/chuck-grassley-native-americans/> Accessed 19 Oct. 2014.
25. ICTMN Staff. "Grassley on VAWA: 'The Non-Indian Doesn't Get a Fair Trial.'" *Indian Country Today Media Network*. Web. 21 Feb. 2013. <http://indiancountrytodaymedianetwork.com/2013/02/21/grassley-vawa-non-indian-doesnt-get-fair-trial-147823> Accessed 01 Oct. 2014.
26. Rob Capriccioso, "U.S. Senator Worries Tribal Courts Will Imprison 'Any American.'" *Indian Country Today Media Network*. Web. 16 Apr. 2012. <http://indiancountrytodaymedianetwork.com/2012/04/16/us-senator-worries-tribal-courts-will-imprison-any-american-108508> Accessed 01 Oct. 2014.
27. For a detailed response to Chuck Grassley's comments, see the National Congress of American Indians' 2013 open letter to Senator Grassley (cited in bibliography).
28. Mulhausen and Villegas, "Violence Against Women Act."
29. *Oliphant v. Suquamish* 115–116.

30. Emile Buchwald, Pamela R. Fletcher and Martha Roth, eds. *Transforming A Rape Culture.* Minneapolis: Milkweed Editions, 2005.
31. Rob Capriccioso, "Tribal Provisions of Women Safety Law."
32. Wang, Hansi Lo. "For Abused Native American Women, New Law Provides A 'Ray Of Hope.'" *National Public Radio.* Web. 20 Feb. 2014. <http://www.npr.org/blogs/codeswitch/2014/02/20/280189261/for-abused-native-american-women-new-law-provides-a-ray-of-hope> Accessed 01 Oct. 2014.
33. Ibid.
34. See Parker and Dina Gilio-Whitaker, "2013 Was a Breakthrough Year for Tribal International Engagement," *Indian Country Today Media Network.* 2014. Web. 01 Jan. 2014. <http://indiancountrytodaymedianetwork.com/2014/01/01/2013-was-breakthrough-year-tribal-international-engagement> Accessed 01 Oct. 2014.
35. Rob Capriccioso, "A Proud Day."
36. Whitaker, "2013 Was a Breakthrough Year for Tribal International Engagement."
37. The United States Attorney's Office, District of Oregon. "Confederated Tribes Of The Umatilla Indian Reservation To Prosecute Domestic Violence Cases Under VAWA 2013 Pilot Project Allows Tribal Prosecution of Non-Indian Abusers For the First Time in More Than Three Decades." Web. 06 Feb. 2014. <http://www.justice.gov/usao/or/news/2014/20140206_vawa.html> Accessed 01 Oct. 2014.
38. S. 47—113th Congress: Violence Against Women Reauthorization Act of 2013.
39. Department of Justice, "VAWA 2013 and Tribal Jurisdiction Over Crimes of Domestic Violence." Web. 06 Feb. 2014. <http://www.justice.gov/sites/default/files/tribal/legacy/2014/02/06/vawa-2013-tribal-jurisdiction-overnon-indian-perpetrators-domes ticviolence.pdf> Accessed 01 Oct. 2014.
40. Steven Perry, "Measuring Crime and Justice in Indian Country," *Bureau of Justice Statistics*: Dec 9, 2004: 9–10.
41. Rob Capriccioso, "A Proud Day."
42. Section 910 of VAWA 2013 was eventually repealed in December 2014 when President Obama signed S. 1474 Public Law 113–275 the Alaska Safe Families and Villages Act of 2014.
43. Rob Capriccioso, "Senate Women Safety Legislation to Exclude 40 Percent of Tribes." *Indian Country Today Media Network.* Web. 24 Apr. 2012. <http://indiancountrytodaymedianetwork.com/2012/04/24/senate-women-safety-legislation-exclude-40-percent-tribes-109930> Accessed 01 Oct. 2014.
44. "Congress Recognizes and Affirms Tribal Courts' Special Domestic Violence Jurisdiction Over Non-Indian Defendants." *Harvard Law Review* (2014): 1518.
45. Ibid., 1517.
46. Ibid.
47. Ibid., 1518.
48. Rob Capriccioso, "A Proud Day."
49. As noted earlier, Section 910 of VAWA 2013 was repealed in December 2014 under S. 1474 Public Law 113–275.

50. Kimberlé Crenshaw, "Mapping the Margins: Intersectionality, Identity Politics, and Violence Against Women of Color." *Stanford Law Review*. 43.6 (1991): 1241–1299.
51. VAWA 2013 prohibits discrimination against the LGBT community. Additionally, it loosens restrictions on U-Visas to protect immigrant women who report domestic violence from deportation. See National Network to End Domestic Violence, "The Violence Against Women Act (VAWA) Renewal Passes the House and Senate and Signed into Law." 2013.
52. "Rep. Marsha Blackburn (R-TN) Opposed VAWA Because It Helped Too Many 'Different Groups.'" YouTube. *ThinkProgress*. Web. 4 Mar. 2013. <https://www.youtube.com/watch?v=DAtbkjv2KH0&feature=youtu.be> Accessed 19 Oct. 2014.
53. Gwen Moore, "'Ain't I a Woman?' Gwen Speaks on Including All Women in VAWA." YouTube. *CSpan*. Web. 1 Mar. 2013 <https://www.youtube.com/watch?v=7-x7LVr3PoI> Accessed 01 Oct. 2014.
54. Jane C. Timm, "VAWA Passes House, with Full Protections for LGBT, Native Americans" *MSNBC*. Web. 12 Sept. 2013. <http://www.msnbc.com/morning-joe/vawa-passes-house-full-protections> Accessed 01 Oct. 2014.
55. Kimberly Robertson, *Un-Settling Questions: The Construction of Indigeneity and Violence Against Native Women*, 2012. Diss. U of California, Los Angeles, 2012. Print.
56. See the doctrine of plenary power in Stephen Pevar, *The Rights of Indians and Tribes* (2012): 27, 34, 58–60, 76–77 and 82–83.
57. As quoted in Robertson, *Unsettling Questions*. 136.
58. Ibid.
59. Ibid., 125–126.
60. As quoted in Rebecca Burns, "VAWA: A Victory for Women-But Which Women?" *In These Times*. Web. 28 Feb. 2013. <http://inthesetimes.com/article/14668/vawa_a_victory_for_womenbut_which_women> Accessed 01 Oct. 2014.
61. "Congress Recognizes and Affirms Tribal Courts' Special Domestic Violence Jurisdiction Over Non-Indian Defendants." *Harvard Law Review* 127 (2014): 1518.
62. Charles Hobbs and Tim Seward, "Give Tribes More Control of Justice in Indian Country." *Indian Country Today Media Network*. Web. 17 Aug. 2014. <http://indiancountrytodaymedianetwork.com/2014/08/17/give-tribes-more-control-justice-indian-country> Accessed 01 Oct. 2014.
63. 36-year-old Eloy Figueroa Lopez was the first non-Native person prosecuted by a tribe under Title IX. See: Sari Horwitz, "Arizona Tribe Set to Prosecute First Non-Indian Under a New Law." *Washington Post*. 2014. At the time of writing, a total of twenty-five other non-Native perpetrators have been adjudicated by three Native nations who participated in the initial phase of enhanced jurisdiction under Title IX of VAWA (The Confederated Tribes of the Umatilla Indian Reservation, the Pascua Yaqui Tribe and the Tulalip Tribes). Starting March 2015, special domestic violence jurisdiction will extend to the governments of all federally recognized tribes who implement the requirements stipulated in Title IX. See Jennifer Bendery, "At Last, Violence Against Women Act Lets Tribes Prosecute Non-Native Domestic Abusers," *Huffington Post*. 2015; and Charles Hobbs and Tim Seward, "Give Tribes More Control of Justice in Indian Country" *Indian Country Today Media Network*. 2014.

64. Mathew Fletcher, "Pascua Yaqui Press Release re: VAWA Pilot Program Selection. Pascua Yaqui Tribe Asserts Authority to Prosecute All Persons, Including Non-Indians for Domestic Violence: Local Tribe Among First to Implement Violence Against Women Act Jurisdictional Provisions." *Turtle Talk.* Indigenous Law and Policy Center Blog. Michigan State University College of Law. Web. 7 Feb. 2014. <http://turtletalk.word press.com/2014/02/07/pascua-yaqui-press-release-revawa-pilot-program-selection/> Accessed 01 Oct. 2014.
65. Sarah Deer, "Violence Against Women and Tribal Law." *Indian Country Today Media Network.* Web. 16 Jul. 2012. <http://indiancountrytodaymedianetwork.com/2012/07/16/violence-against-women-and-tribal-law> Accessed 01 Oct. 2014.
66. Ibid.
67. Taiaiake Alfred, "Sovereignty." *Sovereignty Matters*, 2005. ed. Joanne Barker. University of Nebraska Press, 2005.
68. Sarah Deer, "Violence Against Women and Tribal Law."

CHAPTER SEVEN

Differential Consciousness, the Third Space of Sovereignty, and Strategies for Social Change

> And be it farther enacted if any person or persons should undertake to force a woman and did it by force, it shall be left to woman what punishment she should satisfied with to whip or pay what she say it be law [sic].
>
> —From the 1824 Code of the Creek Nation[1]

Because jurisdictional conflicts are informed by colonial histories of both sexual and legal violence, formulating strategies to address them must take a comprehensive decolonial approach. Given what we know about how American jurisdiction shapes the experiences of sexual violence in Indian country, this chapter surveys various solutions to jurisdictional conflicts in order to examine possibilities for social change.

Chapter Two discusses the work of Andrea Smith to highlight the contradiction of using colonial tools to free oneself from colonial oppression.[2] Attention to Smith's argument is important considering the uncritical and hegemonic way that most non-Native legal scholarship frames solutions to jurisdictional conflicts. However, we also know that approaches to addressing sexual violence that deny the legitimacy of working within existing power structures can themselves be marginalizing as well. For example, by insisting that Native women work entirely outside of the prison industrial complex, the Western legal system, and the "non-profit industrial complex," Smith marginalizes Native women who organize with the help of federal grants, push for legislative change, and feel a sense of safety knowing that their perpetrator is incarcerated. Such approaches preclude the development of social change strategies that may at times purposefully leverage colonial institutions as part of a larger decolonial strategy that envisions a future in which these structures do not exist.

While non-Native scholars almost always frame solutions as existing entirely *within* colonial power structures, and some scholars frame solutions as existing entirely *outside* of colonial institutions, many Native women and Native organizations choose to work *both* within *and* outside of competing power structures to exert agency in the face of colonial violence. This both/and approach illustrates the differential consciousness invoked by Native women and Native organizations that strategically navigate existing power structures as part of a larger counter-imperial strategy.[3] For example, Chapters Five and Six show that rather than: (a) completely rejecting the Tribal Law and Order Act and the Violence Against Women Reauthorization Act of 2013 because they are products of the federal government, or (b) fully embracing them despite their clear shortcomings, many Native women are willing to engage these laws as part of a larger struggle which is ultimately decolonial.

Kevin Bruyneel discusses the willingness of Native communities to incorporate a multifaceted approach to social change in his book *The Third Space of Sovereignty*. Commenting on the "you're either in or you're out"[4] dichotomy that often defines discourse on the participation of Native nations in American politics, Bruyneel highlights the both/and approach that characterizes the history of Native decolonial strategies. In *The Third Space*, Bruyneel presents being forced to choose between working entirely *within* or entirely *outside* of colonial power structures as a false choice originating from the Western colonial paradigm itself.[5] Instead of conforming to this "imperial binary," he demonstrates that Native communities have consistently invoked a "back-and-forth politics on the boundaries working against the system as a whole and also working within the system" that "re-visions American boundaries as active locations for the expression of forms of sovereignty and political identity."[6] Bruyneel calls this refusal of the imperial binary and engagement with politics on the boundaries the "third space of sovereignty."

The third space of sovereignty is evident in activism around violence and jurisdictional conflicts when Native women refuse either/or dichotomies in political organizing and instead choose to work *both* within *and* outside of colonial power structures. As political theorist James Tully notes in Bruyneel's work:

> [I]ndigenous peoples resist colonization in two distinct ways: First they struggle against the structure of domination as a whole and for the sake of their freedoms as peoples. Second, they struggle within the structure of domination vis-à-vis techniques

> of government by exercising their freedom of thought and action with the aim of modifying the system in the short-term and transforming it in the long-term.[7]

It is at this tension between short-term and long-term goals that Native women invoke a differential consciousness to strategically navigate our colonized world. In addressing sexual violence and jurisdictional conflicts in Indian country, Native women like Lavetta Elk, Lisa Iyotte, Sarah Deer and others understand that engaging colonial structures within a decolonial anti-violence movement is not a zero-sum game. Instead, federal institutions—though hegemonic—may still be useful as short-term strategies that work towards long-term goals of liberation. In engaging with a "politics on the boundaries," Native women activists invoke a third space of sovereignty to use existing power structures to shape a future in which these structures may not exist. For example, though using treaties to sue the federal government for sexual assault will not *itself* solve sexual violence, the resources gained from these lawsuits can be used in a long-term struggle that addresses sexual violence as part of a decolonial strategy. While the Tribal Law and Order Act and the Violence Against Women Reauthorization Act of 2013 do not completely dismantle the colonial power structures that created jurisdictional conflicts, resources gained from these laws and national attention to the problem can be used as one of many steps in shaping a future free from legal and sexual violence.

From the perspective of the third space of sovereignty, we can theorize the way that many Native women and Native organizations refuse imperial binaries to exert agency in the face of sexual violence. For example, Sacred Circle—a South Dakota Native women's coalition to end sexual violence in Indian country—situates its anti-violence campaign within long-term decolonial goals, while also employing short-term goals that may at times include colonial institutions. At the *Women Are Sacred* conference I attended in June 2009, Sacred Circle sponsored three days of anti-violence workshops for Native women, Native community organizations, and service providers to Native women.[8] Events included development workshops that helped Native organizations secure federal grants and 501(c)3 status, legal workshops that educated advocates in Indian country on how to navigate jurisdiction in order to ensure that perpetrators are arrested and prosecuted,[9] as well as workshops that taught participants about the colonial context of sexual violence and how long-term anti-violence strategies need to strive for decolonization.[10] In doing so, Sacred Circle educated Native women and Native organizations as to how they could garner federal funding and manage existing laws to fight for justice in the short-term while *simultaneously* showing them how to use these resources within a long-term struggle against colonization as a whole. By engaging federal funding towards a decolonial end, the Native cohort behind Sacred Circle embodied a differential consciousness as they crafted anti-violence approaches to address the needs of Native women.

Like Sacred Circle, the White Buffalo Calf Woman Society (WBCWS) is another program that embodies a differential consciousness in their anti-violence strategies. While working within the non-profit framework, the WBCWS leverages funding from federal grants to engage with short-term strategies that have decolonial long-term goals. In doing so, the WBCWS acknowledges that addressing sexual violence against Native women in Indian country requires engaging existing power structures while simultaneously organizing for a future that does not include them. As the WBCWS's mission statement reads:

> We do not define violence against indigenous women as a problem within a relationship or as the pathology of an individual perpetrator. Again, it is perpetrated and maintained through society and institutions [...] We are committed to providing shelter and advocacy for individuals victimized by violence. We recognize the necessity of a multi-faceted approach—the need to develop an effective response to systems in our community such as health, criminal justice, and other institutions that minimize violence against woman [sic].[11]

The mission statement goes on to say:

> At the same time, we recognize that responding to systems may or may not make significant institutional changes that will stop violence against women. Therefore, we are also dedicated to exploring and creating actions that will move us toward a social transformation that will allow equity for women.[12]

Here the WBCWS recognizes that sexual violence against Native women in Indian country is part of a colonial pathology in which legal and sexual violence are enmeshed. As such, their strategies realize that lasting solutions must focus on addressing the colonial context of sexual violence. However, despite realizing that permanent solutions must exist outside of colonial institutions, the WBCWS invokes a differential consciousness by strategically leveraging these power structures for both short-term and long-term goals. As a federally funded organization, the WBCWS takes advantage of resources from the federal government to implement its future decolonial goals. At the same time, it recognizes that while striving for a decolonial future, it is also valuable to work within other institutions to help manage the epidemic of sexual violence as part of their immediate goals of providing safety, healing, and justice for Native women.

The work of Lavetta Elk, Sacred Circle, and the White Buffalo Calf Woman Society are just a few examples of the multifaceted approach that many Native women and Native community organizations take when responding to jurisdictional conflicts in the prosecution of sexual violence in Indian country. Because Native women and Native community organizations recognize that sexual violence in Indian country arises as the product of colonial violence, Native women craft strategies to address jurisdictional conflicts that take a comprehensive approach. In doing so, these activists work towards addressing the most pressing needs of their constituents while simultaneously working to dismantle the colonial origins of violence against Native women.

What Is Justice?

In Chapter One, I problematized notions of "justice," referencing Jacqueline Agtuca to demonstrate that "justice" must ultimately come from Native women themselves. So while there is value in highlighting the ways that various scholars view solutions to jurisdictional conflicts and sexual violence against Native women, we must always ground this discussion in the diverse experiences of Native women who resist and survive sexual violence themselves. While non-Native legal scholars often theorize justice as existing within the American criminal justice system, and some Native scholars fundamentally deny the legitimacy of the American criminal justice system in its entirety, few scholars are willing to accept that justice might take different forms for different women. By centering the experience of each survivor and acknowledging that each of her visions of justice is valuable and legitimate, we can move towards a notion of "justice" that truly empowers all women.

Sarah Deer (Muscogee Creek) is one of the few scholars and activists that truly center the diverse articulations of justice for Native women in their scholarship. Here, rather than focus on the structures that Native women should or should not use when resisting sexual violence, or telling Native women what justice should look like for them, Sarah Deer proffers the radical notion that we should simply ask them.

In her essay "What She Say, It Be Law," Deer describes the process of researching her own nation's laws and policies around sexual violence. Her findings reveal one of the first written laws of the Creek Nation that reads: "And be it farther enacted if any person or persons should undertake to force a woman and did it by force, it shall be left to woman what punishment she should satisfied with to whip or pay *what she say it be law* [sic]" (my emphasis).[13] Demonstrating the survivor-centered approach of traditional Native jurisprudence, we see a radical idea vis-à-vis the Western criminal justice system and contemporary academic discourse. Rather than passing laws based on what Western culture sees as "justice," and rather than telling women which institutions should ultimately provide justice for them, we need to honor the diverse experiences and visions for justice as articulated by Native women themselves. In the case of the Creek Nation, the traditional Native response to sexual violence against women was to shape law around individual experiences, rather than to force individual experiences to conform to existing laws. As Creek National law indicates, whether the survivor saw justice as physical punishment ("whip"), financial reparations ("pay"), or something else, "it shall be left to [the] woman" to decide. Here, whatever the survivor decided was just, would then become law.

Incorporating "what she say" into the way that we view "justice" in the face of incredible injustice in Indian country is vital in our understanding of agency and formulating strategies for change. In doing so, we can begin to honor the experiences of Native women who articulate "justice" in multiple ways. Often justice, safety, and healing are portrayed as a combination of many things including using the Western criminal justice system to incarcerate perpetrators, using the Western court system to obtain reparations for sexual assault, organizing for legislative change, as well as developing decolonial strategies that subvert existing power structures. And, as we craft anti-violence strategies in the face of jurisdictional conflicts in the prosecution of sexual violence against Native women in Indian country, we need to recognize that the best solutions come from honoring Native women themselves.

Conclusion

Today, Indian country is governed by a complex system of jurisdictional authority whose structure systematically denies justice to Native women. Because of the conflicts created from this jurisdictional authority, sexual assault against Native women in Indian country often goes without investigation, arrest, or prosecution.

This climate of criminal impunity in Indian country is highly racialized, privileging non-Native identity while simultaneously oppressing Native identity. Though tribal justice systems are often the only law enforcement agencies for hundreds of miles, many non-Native people—by virtue of their racial identities, relationships to their victims, and relationships to Indian country—are legally immune from their jurisdiction. At the same time, Native people—by virtue of *their* racial identities—become prime targets for crime in Indian country. While determining jurisdiction in crimes against non-Native people in Indian country is relatively straightforward, when a Native person is assaulted, current jurisdictional law signals the involvement of several sovereign entities. When these sovereign entities become involved, the ability of each to successfully adjudicate crime is compromised. As a result, arrests are rarely made and criminals are rarely prosecuted, creating legal impunity for offenses committed against Native people in particular.

Jurisdictional conflicts in Indian country are also extremely gendered. While identity politics are exploited by myriad non-Native criminals in these spaces, nowhere does it occur more frequently than in the case of non-Native men who perpetrate sexual violence against Native women. Here, Indian country becomes a site of "rape tourism" in which non-Native men specifically prey on Native women because they are confident that there is little anyone can do to stop them.

Jurisdictional authority and legal impunity in Indian country have shaped the epidemic rates of sexual violence against Native women. Today Native women experience rates of sexual violence that far exceed any other demographic in the United States. And, while sexual assault in the non-Native community is an overwhelmingly intra-racial crime, the Native community is the one striking exception. Today one in three Native women can expect to be raped in her lifetime, the majority of whom will experience their assault at the hands of a white man.

Referencing this disturbing reality, President Obama has appeared to genuinely support Native women in Indian country. To show his commitment to Native women and communities, he gave his full-fledged support of the Tribal Law and Order Act of 2010. Preparing to sign the bill into law, he noted that all Americans, even those living on remote reservations, deserve to "enjoy the fullest protections of our laws."[14] While President Obama appeared to address sexual violence against Native women in earnest, like many other non-Native people, he presented additional federal regulations as the solution to jurisdictional conflicts and sexual violence. By portraying American law as a sanctuary for Native women in Indian country, President Obama fails to consider the ways that "our laws" themselves are the foundation for hundreds of years of violence against Native people.

As this work has shown, jurisdictional conflicts (and the race-based privilege for non-Native men in Indian country that they create) are direct products of federal Indian policy itself. The Major Crimes Act, the Dawes General Allotment Act, Public Law 280, and *Oliphant v. Suquamish Indian Tribe* have directly led to the creation and maintenance of jurisdictional conflicts today. These laws were created from the Euro-American fear of Native savagery and lawlessness that has ironically created a very real sense of lawlessness in Indian country. Stemming from a persistent need to remedy the "Indian problem," each of these laws is characterized by civilizing narratives of paternalism, investments in white American hegemony, and divestments in Native sovereignty. As such, the emergence of jurisdictional conflicts from this structure is itself part of the colonial narrative.

When sexual predators exploit jurisdiction in Indian country, paternalism, American hegemony, and cultural genocide are thus written into these assaults.

In addition to law, since first contact, sexual violence against Native women has been a central tool in the war against Native people as a whole. Threatened by the powerful roles Native women played in their communities and in need of constructing Native people as subhuman to legitimate the theft of their land, Native women were constructed as hypersexual and dirty and therefore rapable and violable. Recognizing that they could control entire communities through instituting patriarchy, colonizers inscribed sexual violence to impose hierarchies into non-hierarchical people. And, seeing Native women's fertility as a supreme threat to American hegemony, wholesale sexual and reproductive violence against Native women was centered as a colonial tool.

As sexual violence became part of federal policy, so too did law become structured by sexual violence. It is through both sexual and legal violence that the colonization of the Americas has been possible, and it is at the confluence of both sexual and legal violence that we find jurisdictional conflicts in the prosecution of sexual violence against Native women in Indian country today. Today, when a non-Native man crosses an invisible line to enter Indian country, he enters a colonial space whose very construction depended on the large-scale rape of Native women by white men. Therefore, when this non-Native man specifically targets a Native woman for rape because federal Indian policy privileges his identity while marginalizing hers, we cannot read this assault in a vacuum. Instead, non-Native men who travel to Indian country to prey upon the bodies of Native women perform the entire narrative of colonization. It is because of a colonial history of both sexual violence and legal violence that he is again able to continue to inscribe sexual violence with legal impunity. In this way, jurisdictional conflicts are not only legacies of colonial violence, but actively maintain and inscribe colonial violence on the bodies of Native women and Native communities as a whole.

Though identity politics have been used as a means to disenfranchise Native women in Indian country, the same identities that have been the most marginalized under current jurisdictional laws are also sites of resistance and agency that are creating real social change. For example, while Lavetta Elk was *targeted* for her identity as a Native woman, it is specifically *because* of her identity that she was able to successfully sue the United States for damages. Though suing the federal government for an assault that already happened is not a comprehensive solution to sexual violence against Native women, the ruling in *Elk v. U.S.* can be a powerful tool in the larger movement for justice. *Elk* paves the way for other Native individuals to sue for damages while demonstrating the possibility of being vindicated by the Western legal system. And, significantly, Lavetta Elk reminds the American public that Native people have never passively accepted their own oppression. *Elk v. U.S.* has put the federal government on notice that Native women are pushing back today with the strength of past generations to fight for justice as they always have. For Lavetta Elk, when the federal government and U.S. military blocked her path towards justice, she made her own way. And it is that spirit of resourcefulness, resistance and agency that continues to characterize Native anti-violence strategies vis-à-vis the American settler-state.

While Native women have frequently been constructed as passive subjects who fall victim to a federal Indian policy that is beyond their control, this book demonstrates that Native women do not only survive sexual assault, but go on to organize, resist and shape their own lives despite it. While jurisdictional conflicts have systemically inscribed racialized and gendered oppression, it is at the intersection of race and gender that we find some of the most powerful challenges to colonial violence today. Today, Native women are organizing together to resist, subvert, and shape jurisdictional authority in Indian country in a comprehensive Indigenous anti-violence movement. Here, Native women work together to construct a multifaceted approach to addressing jurisdictional conflicts and sexual violence in the short-term while engaging in long-term decolonial struggles.

While "justice" can mean different things to different Native women and community members, the Native anti-violence struggle—in its ability and willingness to engage in a comprehensive approach with a differential consciousness—demonstrates a willingness to accept that justice is not simply "incarceration" or "decolonization." Sometimes it is neither, but often it is both. As Native women engage in third space sovereignty politics, we must all recognize the wisdom of Creek National law. As we envision a future free from sexual and legal violence, we must always be cognizant of the visions and articulations of justice, healing, and safety that come from Native women themselves. As we shape solutions to jurisdictional conflicts in the prosecution of sexual violence against Native women, we must honor the notion that "what she say" should always form the foundation and inform the approaches of addressing injustice in Indian country.

Notes

1. As quoted in Sarah Deer, "What She Say, It Be Law." *Mending the Sacred Hoop Newsletter*. 4.2 (2000): 1. Deer notes that this law was written by Chief Chilly McIntosh and "reflect[s] that he was still learning English." (See Deer's note 2).
2. See Smith, *Conquest* and Andrea Smith's contributions in INCITE!, *The Color of Violence* and *The Revolution Will Not Be Funded.*
3. I borrow the term "both/and" from the work of Andrew Jolivette (Opelousa/Atakapa-Ishak) with permission. See Andrew Jolivette, "Critical Mixed Race Studies: The Intersections of Identity and Social Justice," *Sociologists in Action: Sociology, Social Change, and Social Justice*. 2nd edition. eds. Kathleen Odell Korgen, Jonathan M. White, Shelley K. White (Thousand Oaks: Sage Publications, 2014).
4. Bruyneel, *The Third Space* xi–xii.
5. Ibid., 21.
6. Ibid.
7. Ibid.
8. *Women Are Sacred Conference: Honoring Sacred Turtle Women*. Sacred Circle. Oakland, CA. 12–14 Jun. 2009.
9. See the following *Women Are Sacred Conference* workshops: Bonnie Clairmont, "Tribal Law and Policy Institute Sexual Assault Resources and Programming" 13 Jun. 2009; Jerry Gardner, "Tribal Legal Resources I" 12 Jun. 2009 and "Tribal Legal Resources II" 13 Jun. 2009; Jacqueline Agtuca, "Understanding the Process to Make Native Women Safe" 14 Jun. 2009.
10. See the following workshops: Roe Bubar and Donna Rouner, "Intersectionality of Violence" 13 Jun. 2009; Elena Giacci, "The Dynamics of Sexual Violence" 12 Jun. 2009; Terri Henry, "Advocacy & Organizing to Create Social Change" 13 Jun. 2009.
11. "Our Mission Statement," *White Buffalo Calf Woman Society, Inc.* Web. <http://www.wbcws.org/index_files/Page371.htm> Accessed 12 Apr. 2011.
12. Ibid.
13. Deer, "What She Say, It Be Law" 1.
14. Obama, "Remarks By the President."

Appendix A: Glossary of Terms

Differential Consciousness Based on the work of Chela Sandoval, the approach of social agents who navigate oppositional power structures with a willingness to engage in multiple and sometimes conflicting strategies for social change.

Federal Indian Policy The body of law that governs the colonial relationship between Native nations and the United States of America. Federal Indian policy includes laws, executive orders, treaties with Native nations, and U.S. Supreme Court cases.

Imperial Binary The false choice offered by colonial institutions in which Indigenous peoples are asked to choose to either operate entirely within or entirely outside of colonial power structures. See Kevin Bruyneel's *The Third Space of Sovereignty*.

Indian Country A legal term defined by the federal government as consisting of "all land within the limits of any Indian reservation under the jurisdiction of the United States government." This definition also includes land within the bounds of other dependent Indian communities including pueblos and rancherias, as well as Indian allotments and Indian titles to lands outside of reservations. See 18 U.S.C. § 1151.

Indian Problem — The problematic social, political, and physical spaces that Native people occupy vis-à-vis the U.S. federal government. The "Indian problem" views Native people and communities as: pre-existing sovereign nations that threaten U.S. political hegemony; physical bodies who stand between the federal government and complete colonization of Native resources; and communities that have survived as distinct social and cultural entities despite assimilationist efforts.

Jurisdiction — The authority of a governing entity to administer justice. In Indian country, there are several sovereign entities that may at times simultaneously vie for jurisdictional authority, and at other times neglect to exercise jurisdiction because of real or perceived limitations.

Jurisdictional Conflict — Any instance in which overlapping or competing authority by federal, state, and/or tribal entities delays or denies justice to a Native woman who has experienced sexual violence. This includes occasions in which multiple entities compete for jurisdiction, compromising the investigation of each, as well as instances in which no entity exercises jurisdiction.

Legal Violence — Legal actions which cause destruction, pain, or suffering. Often describes the use of federal Indian policy to annihilate or assimilate Native people and divest Native communities of their inherent sovereignty.

Native — A term that describes the people and communities Indigenous to the Americas before the arrival of Europeans. This can refer to individuals (e.g. Native woman, Native man) or to distinct pre-existing communities (e.g. Native nation). Used in contrast to "Indian" and "tribe."

Predatory Violence Violence characterized by specifically targeting others. In the context of this research, any instance in which a non-Native man specifically targets a Native women for violence with the intent to exploit identity politics to avoid prosecution.

Sexual Violence Violence which causes destruction, pain, or suffering by forced or coerced actions of a sexual nature. Often describes the attempted or completed rape of one person by another, but also includes violence of a sexual nature initiated by or against communities as a whole. Examples of the latter include forced or coerced sterilization, as well as the figurative rape of the land.

Sovereignty The ability to exert meaningful control over one's own land, body, and resources without unwanted outside influence.

Third Space of Sovereignty From the work of Kevin Bruyneel, the theory that Native communities have always refused binary notions of political identity and social change, and instead invoke an alternative "third space" when negotiating their relationships with colonial power structures. This term may also refer to the space that Native nations occupy vis-à-vis the federal government as not completely within, but also not completely outside of the U.S. political sphere.

Appendix B: Law and Policy Reference

Fort Laramie Treaty of 1868 15 Stat. 635	1868 treaty guaranteeing land ownership, hunting rights, and jurisdictional authority among other things. Includes the "bad men" clause that protects Native beneficiaries from the violence of "bad men among the whites."
Ex Parte Crow Dog *(Crow Dog)* 109 U.S. 556	1883 U.S. Supreme Court decision that returned jurisdiction over Crow Dog to the Lakota Nation after the murder of Spotted Tail.
Major Crimes Act (MCA) 18 U.S.C. § 1153	1885 federal law extending federal jurisdiction over "major crimes" committed in Indian country. Major crimes include murder, rape, kidnapping and arson among others.
General Allotment Act (Dawes Act) 25 U.S.C. § 331–358	1887 federal law that divided communal Native landholdings into individual parcels that were then distributed to individual Indian people. After disbursement, "surplus" land was seized by the federal government.

Public Law 280 (PL 280) 18 U.S.C. § 1162	1953 federal law passed during the Termination Era. This law forced six states to assume jurisdiction over crimes committed in Indian country while allowing many other states to opt in (and out) of state jurisdiction.
Indian Civil Rights Act (ICRA) 25 U.S.C. § 1301–1303	1968 federal law that imposes mandatory sentencing limitations on tribal courts, among other things. Upon its passage, the ICRA limited tribal courts to imposing a $500 fine and 6 months in jail for any single offense. This act was amended in 1986 to a $5,000 fine and 1 year in jail, and in 2010 to a $15,000 fine and 3 years in jail.
Oliphant v. Suquamish Indian Tribe *(Oliphant)* 435 U.S. 191 (1978)	1978 U.S. Supreme Court case whose ruling prohibited Native nations from prosecuting non-Native perpetrators of crime in Indian country.
Lavetta Elk v. the United States *(Elk v. U.S.)* No. 05–186L	2009 civil case tried in U.S. federal court concerning a non-Native army recruiter who sexually assaulted a Native woman in Indian country. The judge awarded the plaintiff significant financial compensation under the "bad men" clause of the Fort Laramie Treaty of 1868.
Tribal Law and Order Act (TLOA) Pub L. No 111-211	2010 federal law that attempts to address jurisdictional conflicts and sexual violence against Native women by increasing communication between tribal, state and federal entities, and by making grants available to tribal governments, among other things.
Violence Against Women Reauthorization Act of 2013 (VAWA 2013) S. 47 113th Congress	2013 reauthorization of the Violence Against Women Act, which includes enhanced protections for Native women, immigrant women, and the LGBT community. Title IX: "Safety for Indian Women" extends "special domestic violence jurisdiction" to tribes over non-Native perpetrators in limited cases.

Bibliography

'111th Congress: Statistically Speaking' *CQ Today*. 6 Nov. 2008. Web. 12 Apr. 2011 <www.cq.com/graphics/monitor/.../mon20081105-5election-stats.pdf>

Agtuca, Jacqueline. 'Beloved Women: Life Givers, Caretakers, Teachers of Future Generations.' *Sharing Our Stories of Survival*. Eds. Sarah Deer, Bonnie Clairmont, Carrie A. Martell and Maureen L. White Eagle. New York: Altamira Press, 2007.

———. 'Understanding the Process to Make Native Women Safe.' *Women Are Sacred Conference: Honoring Sacred Turtle Women*. Sacred Circle. Oakland, CA: 14 Jun. 2009.

Alaska Safe Families and Villages Act of 2014. Public Law: 113–275 (2014) (enacted). Print.

Alfred, Taiaiake. 'Sovereignty.' *Sovereignty Matters*. Ed. Joanne Barker. Lincoln: University of Nebraska Press, 2005.

Allen, Paula Gunn. 'Violence and the American Indian Woman.' *The Speaking Profits Us: Violence in the Lives of Women of Color.* Ed. Maryviolet C. Burns. Seattle: Center for the Prevention of Sexual and Domestic Violence, 1986.

Amnesty International. *Maze of Injustice: The Failure to Protect Indigenous Women from Sexual Violence in the USA.* New York: Amnesty International Publications, 2007.

———. *Maze of Injustice: The Failure to Protect Indigenous Women from Sexual Violence in the USA: One Year Update*. New York: Amnesty International Publications, 2008.

Baca, Alexandria. 'Sen. John Cornyn Cites Tribal Provision in Vote Against Anti-violence Bill.' Trail Blazers Blog. *Dallas News*, 13 Feb. 2013. Web. 01 Oct. 2014. <http://trailblazersblog.dallasnews.com/2013/02/sen-cornyn-votes-against-anti-violence-bill-cites-unconstitutional-amendment.html/>

Bachman, Ronet, Heather Zaykowski, Rachel Kallmyer, Margarita Poteyeva and Christina Lanier. *Violence Against American Indians and Alaska Native Women and the Criminal Justice Response: What is Known*. U.S. Department of Justice. 223691. Aug. 2009.

Barker, Joanne. 'For Whom Sovereignty Matters.' *Sovereignty Matters*. Ed. Joanne Barker. Lincoln: University of Nebraska Press, 2005.

Bendery, Jennifer. 'At Last, Violence Against Women Act Lets Tribes Prosecute Non-Native Domestic Abusers.' *Huffington Post*. 06 Mar. 2015. Web. 07 Mar. 2015. < http://www.huffingtonpost.com/2015/03/06/vawa-native-americans_n_6819526.html>

Biolsi, Thomas. 'Imagined Geographies: Sovereignty, Indigenous Space, and American Indian Struggle.' *American Ethnologist*. 32.2 (2005): 239–259.

Brown, Dee. *Bury My Heart At Wounded Knee: An Indian History of the American West*. New York: Holt, Rinehart &Winston, 1970.

Bruyneel, Kevin. *The Third Space of Sovereignty: The Postcolonial Politics of U.S.–Indigenous Relations*. Minneapolis: University of Minnesota Press, 2007.

Bubar, Roe, and Donna Rouner. 'Intersectionality of Violence.' *Women Are Sacred Conference: Honoring Sacred Turtle Women*. Sacred Circle. Oakland, CA. 13 Jun. 2009.

Buchwald, Emile, Pamela R. Fletcher and Martha Roth, eds. *Transforming A Rape Culture, Revised Edition*. Minneapolis: Milkweed Editions, 2005.

Burns, Rebecca. VAWA: A Victory for Women-But Which Women?" *In These Times*. 28 Feb. 2013. Web. 01 Oct. 2014. <http://inthesetimes.com/article/14668/vawa_a_victory_for_womenbut_which_women>

Cantwell, Maria. 'In Floor Speech, Cantwell Urges Swift Passage of Violence Against Women Act with Strong Tribal Provisions.' Maria Cantwell, United States Senator for Washington. 7 Feb. 2013. Web. 01 Oct. 2014. <http://www.cantwell.senate.gov/public/index.cfm/2013/2/in-floor-speech-cantwell-urges-swift-passage-of-violence-against-women-act-with-strong-tribal-provisions>

Capriccioso, Rob. 'A Proud Day for Tribal Advocates of the Violence Against Women Act' *Indian Country Today Media Network*. 28 Feb. 2013. Web. 01 Oct. 2014. <http://indiancountrytodaymedianetwork.com/2013/02/28/proud-day-tribal-advocates-violence-against-women-act-147932>

———. 'House Republican VAWA Bill Offers Strong Tribal Protections; Will Cantor Accept?' *Indian Country Today Media Network*. 22 Feb. 2013. Web. 01 Oct. 2014. <http://indiancountrytodaymedianetwork.com/2013/02/22/house-republican-vawa-bill-offers-strong-tribal-protections-will-cantor-accept-147851>

———.'Senate Women Safety Legislation to Exclude 40 Percent of Tribes' *Indian Country Today Media Network*. 24 Apr. 2012. Web. 01 Oct. 2014. <http://indiancountrytodaymedianetwork.com/2012/04/24/senate-women-safety-legislation-exclude-40-percent-tribes-109930>

———.'Tribal Law and Order Act Costly.' *Tribune Business News*. 28 Jul. 2010.

———.'Tribal Provisions of Women Safety Law Under Senate Attack.' *Indian Country Today Media Network*. 01 Apr. 2012. Web. 01 Oct. 2014. <http://indiancountrytodaymedianetwork.com/2012/04/01/tribal-provisions-women-safety-law-under-senate-attack-105634>

———. 'U.S. Senator Worries Tribal Courts Will Imprison 'Any American." *Indian Country Today Media Network*. 16 Apr. 2012. Web. 01 Oct. 2014. <http://indiancountrytodaymedianetwork.com/2012/04/16/us-senator-worries-tribal-courts-will-imprison-any-american-108508>

Casas, Bartolomé De Las. *The Devastation of the Indies: A Brief Account*. Baltimore: The Johns Hopkins University Press, 1992. [Originally published in 1542].

Castañeda, Antonia. 'Sexual Violence in the Politics and Policies of Conquest: Amerindian Women and the Spanish Conquest of Alta California'. *Building with Our Hands: New Directions in Chicana Studies.* Eds. Adela De La Torre and Beatriz M. Pesquera. Berkeley: University of California Press, 1993.

Castleman, David. 'Personal Jurisdiction in Tribal Courts.' *University of Pennsylvania Law Review*. 154.5 (2006): 1253–1282.

Chang, Angela. 'Victory! Tribal Law and Order Act Passes in the US Senate!' *Amnesty International USA Web Log*. 1 Jul. 2010. Web. 12 Apr. 2011. <http://blog.amnestyusa.org/women/victory-tribal-law-and-order-act-passes-in-the-us-senate>

Churchill, Ward. *Perversions of Justice: Indigenous Peoples and Angloamerican Law.* San Francisco: City Lights Books, 2003.

Clairmont, Bonnie. 'Tribal Law and Policy Institute Sexual Assault Resources and Programming.' *Women Are Sacred Conference: Honoring Sacred Turtle Women.* Sacred Circle. Oakland, CA. 13 Jun. 2009.

Cohen, John. *The Four Voyages of Christopher Columbus*. New York: Penguin, 1969.

Collins, Patricia Hill. *Black Feminist Thought, Knowledge, Consciousness, and the Politics of Empowerment*. Boston: Unwin Hyman Inc., 1991.

Condition of the Indian Tribes. Report of the Joint Special Committee. Washington, D.C.: Government Printing Office, 1867.

'Congress Recognizes and Affirms Tribal Courts' Special Domestic Violence Jurisdiction Over Non-Indian Defendants.' *Harvard Law Review* 127 (2014): 1509–518. Print.

Congressional Senate Hearing. 'Examining S. 797, The Tribal Law and Order Act of 2009.' 111th Congress. First Session. Washington, D.C.: GPO, 2009. Print.

Constitution of the United States, Article Six.

Cook, Chuck. 'Rape with Impunity: Police Shrug at 'Non-Emergency' Crime.' *Indian Country Today Media Network.* 7.20 (1987) 11 Nov.

Crenshaw, Kimberlé. 'Mapping the Margins: Intersectionality, Identity Politics, and Violence Against Women of Color.' *Stanford Law Review*. 43.6 (1991): 1241–1299.

Crow Dog, Mary. *Lakota Woman*. New York: Harper Perennial, 1990.

Current TV. *Rape on the Reservation*. Vanguard. Jun. 2010. Video. 4 Oct. 2010. <http://current.com/shows/vanguard/92467753>

Deer, Sarah. 'Federal Indian Law and Violent Crime: Native Women and Children at the Mercy of the State.' *The Color of Violence: The INCITE! Anthology*. Ed. INCITE! Cambridge: South End Press, 2006.

——. 'Violence Against Women and Tribal Law' *Indian Country Today Media Network.* 16 Jul. 2012. Web. 01 Oct. 2014. <http://indiancountrytodaymedianetwork.com/2012/07/16/violence-against-women-and-tribal-law>

———. 'Sovereignty of the Soul: Exploring the Intersection of Rape Law Reform and Federal Indian Law.' *Suffolk University Law Review*. 38 (2005): 455–466.

———. 'What She Say, It Be Law.' *Mending the Sacred Hoop Newsletter*. 4.2 (2000): 1.

Deer, Sarah, and Carrie E. Garrow. *Tribal Criminal Law and Procedure*. New York: Altamira Press. 2007.

Deer, Sarah, Bonnie Clairmont, Carrie A. Martell and Maureen L. White Eagle, eds. *Sharing Our Stories of Survival*. New York: Altamira Press, 2007.

Deloria, Vine, and Clifford Lytle. *American Indians, American Justice*. Austin: University of Texas Press, 1983.

Deloria, Philip. 'From Nation to Neighborhood: Land, Policy, Culture, Colonialism, and Empire in U.S.–Indian Relations.' *The Cultural Turn in U.S. History: Past, Present, and Future*. Eds. James W. Cook, Lawrence B. Glickman, and Michael O'Malley. Chicago: University of Chicago Press, 2008: 343–382.

Department of Justice. 'VAWA 2013 and Tribal Jurisdiction Over Crimes of Domestic Violence.' 06 Feb. 2014. Web. 01 Oct. 2014. <http://www.justice.gov/sites/default/files/tribal/legacy/2014/02/06/vawa-2013-tribal-jurisdiction-overnon-indian-perpetrators-domesticviolence.pdf>.

Donovan, Bill. 'S.D. Court Case May Allow Claims Against the U.S.' *Navajo Times*. 7 May. 2009: A4.

———. 'Police Report Rape, Domestic Violence Cases Up in 2008.' *Navajo Times*. 26 Mar. 2009.

Duthu, Bruce. *American Indians and the Law*. New York: Penguin Group, 2008.

Family Research Council, 'Form letter: Vote 'No' on S. 47.' 1 Feb. 2013.

Fletcher, Matthew L.M. 'Addressing the Epidemic of Domestic Violence in Indian Country by Restoring Tribal Sovereignty.' *American Constitution Society for Law and Policy*. Mar. 2009.

———. "Pascua Yaqui Press Release re: VAWA Pilot Program Selection. Pascua Yaqui Tribe Asserts Authority to Prosecute All Persons, Including Non-Indians for Domestic Violence: Local Tribe Among First to Implement Violence Against Women Act Jurisdictional Provisions." Turtle Talk. Indigenous Law and Policy Center Blog. Michigan State University College of Law. 7 Feb. 2014. Web. 01 Oct. 2014 <http://turtletalk.word press.com/2014/02/07/pascua-yaqui-press-release-re-vawa-pilot-program-selection/>

———. 'Rethinking Customary Law in Tribal Court Jurisprudence.' *Michigan State University College of Law: Indigenous Law and Policy Center Occasion Paper Series*. Indigenous Law and Policy Center Working Paper 2006–04. Nov. 2006.

Fordyce, Jeanette. 'Safe Women, Strong Nations Project Combats Rape on Reservations.' *Twin Cities Daily Planet*. 3 Aug. 2010. Web. 01 Oct. 2014. <http://www.tcdailyplanet.net/news/2010/08/02/safe-women-strong-nations-project>

'Forging a New and Better Future Together: 2010 White House Tribal Nations Conference Progress Report.' The White House. 23 Jun. 2010. Print.

Fort Laramie Treaty. 15 Stat. 635. 29 Apr. 1868.

Gardner, Jerry. 'Tribal Legal Resources I.' *Women Are Sacred Conference: Honoring Sacred Turtle Women*. Sacred Circle. Oakland, CA. 12 Jun. 2009.

———. 'Tribal Legal Resources II.' *Women Are Sacred Conference: Honoring Sacred Turtle Women.* Sacred Circle. Oakland, CA. 13 Jun. 2009.

Garrigan, Mary. 'Program Targets Crime In Tribal Communities.' *Rapid City Journal.* 5 Aug. 2010.

Giacci, Elena. 'The Dynamics of Sexual Violence.' *Women Are Sacred Conference: Honoring Sacred Turtle Women.* Sacred Circle. Oakland, CA. 12 Jun. 2009.

Gilbert, Craig. 'Sen. Ron Johnson Calls Violence Against Women Bill Unconstitutional—JSOnline.' *Journal Sentinel,* 13 Feb. 2013. Web. 19 Oct. 2014. <http://www.jsonline.com/blogs/news/191035431.html>

Gilio-Whitaker, Dina. '2013 Was a Breakthrough Year for Tribal International Engagement' *Indian Country Today Media Network.* 01 Jan. 2014. Web. 01 Oct. 2014. < http://indiancountrytodaymedianetwork.com/2014/01/01/2013-was-breakthrough-year-tribal-international-engagement>

Gold, Jenny. 'Bill Bolsters Tribal Power to Prosecute Rape Cases.' *National Public Radio.* 23 Jul. 2008.

Goldberg, Carole E. 'Public Law 280.' *American Indian Treaties Publication.* Los Angeles: University of California, Los Angeles. American Indian Culture and Research Center. Series No. 1, 1975.

Gray, Louis. 'Protecting Indian Women Vital For Native Communities.' *Native American Times.* 14 Oct. 2005.

Green, Rayna. 'The Pocahontas Perplex: The Image of Indian Women in American Culture.' *Massachusetts Review.* 16.4 (1975): 698–714.

Gruchow, Matthew. 'Native Woman Wins Unprecedented Case.' *Ojibwe News.* 1 May. 2009.

Harring, Sidney. 'Crow Dog and the Western Justice System.' *Tribal Criminal Law and Procedure.* Eds. Sarah Deer and Carrie E. Garrow. New York: Altamira Press, 2007.

———. *Crow Dog's Case: American Indian Sovereignty, Tribal Law, and United States Law in the Nineteenth Century.* Cambridge: Cambridge University Press, 1994.

Helton, Taiawagi, and Lindsay G. Robertson. 'The Foundations of Federal Indian Law and Its Application in the Twentieth Century.' *Beyond Red Power: American Indian Politics and Activism Since 1900.* Eds. Daniel M. Cobb and Loretta Fowler. Santa Fe: School for Advanced Research Press, 2007.

Henry, Terri. 'Advocacy & Organizing to Create Social Change.' *Women Are Sacred Conference: Honoring Sacred Turtle Women.* Sacred Circle. Oakland, CA. 13 Jun. 2009.

Hernández-Avila, Inés. 'In Praise of Insubordination, Or, What Makes a Good Woman Go Bad?' *Chicana Cultural Studies Reader.* Ed. Angie Chabram-Dernersesian. New York: Routledge, 2006.

Hill, Brenda. 'The Role of Advocates in the Tribal Legal System.' *Sharing Our Stories of Survival.* Eds. Sarah Deer, Bonnie Clairmont, Carrie A. Martell and Maureen L. White Eagle. New York: Altamira Press, 2007.

Hobbs, Charles and Tim Seward. 'Give Tribes More Control of Justice in Indian Country.' Indian Country Today Media Network.com. *Indian Country Today Media Network,* 17 Aug. 2014. Web. 01 Oct. 2014. <http://indiancountrytodaymedianetwork.com/2014/08/17/give-tribes-more-control-justice-indian-country>

Horwitz, Sari. 'Arizona Tribe Set to Prosecute First Non-Indian under a New Law.' *Washington Post.* 18 Apr. 2014. Web. 01 Oct. 2014. <http://www.washingtonpost.com/national/arizona-tribe-set-to-prosecute-first-non-indian-under-a-new-law/2014/04/18/127a202a-bf20-11e3-bcec-b71ee10e9bc3_story.html>

Hurtado, Albert. 'When Strangers Met: Sex and Gender on Three Frontiers.' *Frontiers.* 17.2 (1996): 52–74.

INCITE! Women of Color Against Violence, ed. *The Color of Violence: The INCITE! Anthology.* Cambridge: South End Press, 2006.

———. *The Revolution Will Not Be Funded: Beyond the Non-Profit Industrial Complex.* Cambridge: South End Press, 2007.

ICTMN Staff. 'Grassley on VAWA: 'The Non-Indian Doesn't Get a Fair Trial'' *Indian Country Today Media Network.* 21 Feb. 2013. Web. 01 Oct. 2014. <http://indiancountrytodaymedianetwork.com/2013/02/21/grassley-vawa-non-indian-doesnt-get-fair-trial-147823>

Iyotte, Lisa. 'Remarks Before Signing of the Tribal Law and Order Act.' The White House. Washington, D.C. 29 Jul. 2010. Video. 12 Apr. 2011. <http://www.whitehouse.gov/blog/2010/07/29/tribal-law-and-order-act-2010-a-step-forward-native-women>

Jeffredo-Warden, Louis V. 'Perceiving, Experiencing, and Expressing the Sacred: An Indigenous Southern Californian View,' *Over the Edge: Remapping the American West,* Eds. Valerie J. Matsumoto and Blake Allmendinger. London: University of California Press, 1999.

Jennings, Francis. 'Virgin Land and Savage People.' *American Quarterly* 23.4 (1971): 519–541.

Jimenez, Vanessa J., and Soo C. Song. 'Concurrent Tribal and State Jurisdiction Under Public Law 280.' *The American University Law Review.* 47.1627 (1998): 1627–1707.

Jimson, Thomas. *Reflections on Manifest Destiny and Race.* Center for World Indigenous Studies. 1992 Web. 12 Apr. 2011 <www.cwis.org/fwdp/Americas/manifest.txt>

Johnson, Steven. 'Jurisdiction: Criminal Jurisdiction and Enforcement Problems on Indian Reservations in the Wake of Oliphant.' *American Indian Law Review.* 7.2 (1979): 291–317.

Jolivette, Andrew. 'Critical Mixed Race Studies: The Intersections of Identity and Social Justice,' *Sociologists in Action: Sociology, Social Change, and Social Justice.* 2nd Edition. Kathleen Odell Korgen, Jonathan M. White, Shelley K. White, eds. Thousand Oaks: Sage Publications, 2014.

Kasperowicz, Pete. 'House Passes Violence Against Women Act Reauthorization.' *The Hill.* 16 May 2012. Web. 01 Oct. 2014. <http://thehill.com/blogs/floor-action/house/227877-house-passes-violence-against-women-act-reauthorization>

Kent, Jim. 'Lakota Woman Accuses U.S. Army Recruiter of Sexual Assault; Forfeits Full College Scholarship to 'Live Her Dream.'' *News From Indian Country.* 2 Jun. 2003.

Keyes, Scott. 'Top GOP Senator: Native American Juries Are Incapable Of Trying White People Fairly.' *ThinkProgress.* 21 Feb. 2013. Web. 19 Oct. 2014. <http://thinkprogress.org/justice/2013/02/21/1619501/chuck-grassley-native-americans/>

King, C. Richard. 'De/Scribing Squ*w: Indigenous Women and Imperial Idioms in the United States.' *American Indian Culture and Research Journal.* UCLA American Indian Studies Center. 27.2 (2003): 1–16.

'Lands in Severalty to Indians: Views of the Minority.' *Index to the Reports of Committees of the House of Representatives for the First and Second Sessions of the Forty-Sixth Congress 1879–1880.* Volume 5—Nos. 1521–1793. Washington: D.C.: Government Printing Office, 1880.

Larson, Sidner. 'Making Sense of Federal Indian Law.' *Wicazo Sa Review.* 19.1 (2005): 9–21.

Lavetta Elk v. the United States. No. 05–186L. Apr 28 2009. Print.

Leonhard, M. Brent. 'Closing a Gap in Indian Country Justice: Oliphant, Lara and DOJ's Proposed Fix.' *Harvard Law Journal On Racial & Ethnic Justice* 28 (2012): 117–71.

Loy, Debra. 'Criminal Law: Equal Protection and Unequal Punishment Under the Major Crimes Act: *United States v. Cleveland.*' *American Indian Law Review.* 3.1 (1975): 103–108.

Lujan, Carol, and Gordon Adams. 'U.S. Colonization of Indian Justice Systems: A Brief History.' *Wicazo Sa Review.* 19.2 (2004): 9–23.

Luna-Firebaugh, Eileen. *Tribal Policing: Asserting Sovereignty, Seeking Justice.* Tucson: University of Arizona Press, 2007.

Major Crimes Act. 18 U.S.C. § 1153.

Markham, Clements R. Trans. 'Amerigo Vespucci to Lorenzo Pietro Francesco Di Medici. March (or April) 1503.' *The Letters of Amerigo Vespucci and Other Documents Illustrative of His Career.* New York: Burt Franklin, 2011.

McClelland, Mac. 'A Fistful of Dollars.' *Mother Jones.* Nov-Dec (2010): 64–65.

Meisner, Kevin. 'Modern Problems of Criminal Jurisdiction in Indian Country.' *American Indian Law Review.* 17.1 (1992): 175–207.

Mihesuah, Devon Abbott. *Indigenous American Women: Decolonization, Empowerment, Activism.* Lincoln: University of Nebraska Press, 2003.

Mills, Jonathan, and Kara Brown. 'Law Enforcement in Indian Country: The Struggle for a Solution.' 1 Nov. 2002. Web. 12 Apr. 2011. <uchastings.edu/site_files/indiancountry.pdf>

Mohanty, Chandra Talpade. 'Under Western Eyes: Feminist Scholarship and Colonial Discourses.' *Third World Women and the Politics of Feminism.* Chandra Mohanty, Ann Russo and Lourdes Torres, eds., Indianapolis: University of Indiana Press, 1991.

Moore, Gwen. "Ain't I a Woman?' Gwen Speaks on Including All Women in VAWA.' YouTube. *CSpan,* 1 Mar. 2013. Web. 01 Oct. 2014. <https://www.youtube.com/watch?v=7-x7LVr3PoI>

Mulhausen, David B., and Christina Villegas, 'Violence Against Women Act: Reauthorization Fundamentally Flawed.' *Heritage Foundation.* 29 Mar. 2012. Web. 19 Oct. 2014. <http://www.heritage.org/research/reports/2012/03/the-violence-against-women-act-reauthorization-fundamentally-flawed>

National Center on Domestic and Sexual Violence. The National Task Force to End Sexual and Domestic Violence Against Women. 'The Safeguards in the Violence Against Women Act (VAWA),' 2011. Web. 01 Oct. 2014. <http://www.ncdsv.org/images/NatlTFEndSDVAW_Safeguards%20in%20VAWA_2011.pdf>

———. 'Heritage Action is Wrong About its VAWA Claims,' *Huffington Post.* 2013. Web. 01 Oct. 2014 <http://big.assets.huffingtonpost.com/ntf.pdf>

National Congress of American Indians. NCAI Task Force on Violence Against Women. 'Open Letter to the Honorable Chuck Grassley.' 22 Feb. 2013. Web. 01 Oct. 2014. <http://files.

ncai.org/VAWA/NCAI%20VAWA%20Task%20Force%20-%20Letter%20to%20Grassley%20-%20Final.pdf>

Ned-Sunnyboy, Eleanor. 'Special Issues Facing Alaska Native Women Survivors of Violence.' *Sharing Our Stories of Survival.* Eds. Sarah Deer, Bonnie Clairmont, Carrie A. Martell and Maureen L. White Eagle. New York: Altamira Press. 2007.

"No' on the Violence Against Women Act (VAWA).' *Heritage Action for America.* Senate Key Votes, 04 Feb. 2013. Web. 01 Oct. 2014. <http://heritageaction.com/key-votes/no-on-the-violence-against-women-act-vawa/>

Norrell, Brenda. 'Native Women are Prey; Communities and Courts Fail Native Women.' *News From Indian Country.* 27.26 (2009).

Obama, Barack. 'Remarks by the President Before Signing the Tribal Law and Order Act.' Office of the Press Secretary. The White House. 29 Jul. 2010. Print.

Oliphant v. Suquamish Indian Tribe. 435 U.S. 191. 6 Mar. 1978. Print.

'Our Input Still Needed in Law and Order Act.' *Indian Country Today Media Network.* 2 Sep. 2010. Web. 12 Apr. 2010 <http://www.indiancountrytoday.com/internal?st=print&id=102101183&path= /opinion.editorials>

'Our Mission Statement.' *White Buffalo Calf Woman Society, Inc.* Web. 12 Apr. 2011.<http://www.wbcws.org/index_files/Page371.htm>

Pember, Mary Annette. 'Tribes Gain New Clout Against Crime.' *Daily Yonder.* 12 Aug. 2010. Web. 12 Apr. 2011. <dailyyonder.com/tribes-gain-new-clout-against-crime/2010/08/11/2884>

Perry, Barbara. *Policing Race and Place in Indian Country: Over-and Underenforcement.* New York: Lexington Books, 2009.

Perry, Steven. 'Measuring Crime and Justice in Indian Country.' *Bureau of Justice Statistics.* Dec 9, 2004: 9–10.

Pevar, Stephen L. *The Rights of Indians and Tribes.* Oxford: Oxford UP, 2012.

———. *The Rights of Indians and Tribes: The Authoritative ACLU Guide to Indian Tribal Rights.* Carbondale: Southern Illinois University Press, 1992.

Pisarello, Lisa. 'Lawless By Design: Jurisdiction, Gender and Justice in Indian Country.' *Emory Law Journal.* 59 (2010): 1515–1552.

Pommersheim, Frank. *Braid of Feathers: American Indian Law and Contemporary Tribal Life.* Berkeley: University of California Press, 1997.

Prygoski, Philip J. 'From Marshall to Marshall: The Supreme Court's Changing Stance on Tribal Sovereignty.' *American Bar Association.* Fall 1995.

Ramirez, Renya. 'Race, Tribal Nation, and Gender: A Native Feminist Approach to Belonging.' *Meridians: Feminism, Race, Transnationalism.* 7.2 (2007): 22–40.

Regan, Sheila. 'Tribal Law and Order Act's XI Addresses Indian Women Sexual Assault Issues.' *Twin Cities Daily Planet.* 27 Oct. 2010. Web. 12 Apr. 2011 <http://www.tcdailyplanet.net/news/2010/10/11/tribal-law-and-order-act%E2%80%99s-xi-addresses-indian-women-sexual-assault-issues>

Report of the Commissioner of Indian Affairs to the Secretary of the Interior. Washington, D.C.: Government Printing Office, 1872.

Rieder, Jonathan. *Gospel of Freedom: Martin Luther King Jr.'s Letter from Birmingham Jail and the Struggle that Changed a Nation*. New York: Bloomsbury Press, 2013.

Reno, Janet. 'A Federal Commitment to Tribal Justice Systems.' (79 Judicature 1995).

'Rep. Marsha Blackburn (R-TN) Opposed VAWA Because It Helped Too Many 'Different Groups" YouTube. *ThinkProgress*, 4 Mar. 2013. Web. 19 Oct. 2014. <https://www.youtube.com/watch?v=DAtbkjv2KH0&feature=youtu.be>

Riley, Michael. 'Promises, Justice Broken: A Dysfunctional System Lets Serious Reservation Crimes Go Unpunished and Puts Indians at Risk.' *Denver Post*. 11 Nov. 2007.

Ritcheske, Kathryn A. 'Liability of Non-Indian Batterers in Indian Country: A Jurisdictional Analysis.' *Texas Journal of Women and the Law*. 14.201 (2005): 201–225.

Robertson, Kimberly. 'Un-Settling Questions: The Construction of Indigeneity and Violence Against Native Women.' Diss. U of California, Los Angeles, 2012. Print.

Rosen, Deborah. 'Colonization Through the Law: The Judicial Defense of State Indian Legislation, 1790–1880.' *American Journal of Legal History*. 46.1 (2004): 26–54.

Ross, Luana. 'From the 'F' Word to Indigenous/Feminisms.' *Wicazo Sa Review*. 24.2 (2009): 39–52.

———. *Inventing the Savage*. Austin: University of Texas Press, 1998.

Russell, Steve. 'Making Peace with Crow Dog's Ghost: Racialized Prosecution in Federal Indian Law.' *Wicazo Sa Review*. (Spring 2006): 61–76.

'S. 47—113th Congress: Violence Against Women Reauthorization Act of 2013.' www.GovTrack.us. 2013. October 19, 2014 <https://www.govtrack.us/congress/bills/113/s47>

Sale, Kirkpatrick. *Christopher Columbus and the Conquest of Paradise*. New York: Alfred Knopf, 1990.

Sandoval, Chela. *Methodology of the Oppressed*. Minneapolis: University of Minnesota Press, 2000.

Sawers, Brian. 'Tribal Land Corporations: Using Incorporation to Combat Fractionation.' *Nebraska Law Review*. 88.2 (2009): 385–482.

Schmelzer, Paul. 'Overdue Indian Crime Bill Passes Without Support of Colo. Republicans.' *Colorado Independent*. 28 Jul. 2010. Web. 12 Apr 2011.<http://coloradoindependent.com/58201/overdue-indian-crime-bill-passes-without-support-of-colo-republicans>

Senate Committee on Indian Affairs. 'Examining S. 797, The Tribal Law and Order Act of 2009.' 111th Congress. First Session. Washington, D.C.: GPO, 2009. Print.

'Sen. Grassley Doesn't Think Native Americans Can Hold Fair Trials.' YouTube. *Think Progress*, 20 Feb. 2013. Web. 19 Oct. 2014. <https://www.youtube.com/watch?v=BRpjxtLrTcE>

'Sexual Assault in Indian Country: Confronting Sexual Violence.' *National Sexual Violence Resource Center*. (2000): 6. Web. 12 Apr. 2011.<http://www.nsvrc.org/_cms/fileUpload/indian.htm>

Singh, Shefali. 'Closing the Gap of Justice: Providing Protection for Native American Women Through the Special Domestic Violence Criminal Jurisdiction Provision of VAWA.' *Columbia Journal of Gender and Law* 28.1 (2014): 197–227. ProQuest. 1 Oct. 2014.

Smith, Andrea. *Conquest: Sexual Violence and American Indian Genocide*. Cambridge: South End Press, 2005.

———. 'Not an Indian Tradition: The Sexual Colonization of Native Peoples.' *Hypatia*.18.2 (Spring 2003): 70–85.

Stannard, David E. *American Holocaust: The Conquest of the New World.* New York: Oxford University Press, 1992.

Sullivan, Laura. 'Legal Hurdles Stall Rape Cases on Native Lands.' *National Public Radio.* 26 Jul. 2007.

———. 'Lawmakers Move to Curb Rape on Native Lands.' *National Public Radio.* 3 May. 2009.

'Summary of the Tribal Law and Order Act.' *United States Senate Committee on Indian Affairs.* Mar. 2009. Web. *4 Oct. 2010.* <www.indian.senate.gov/public/_files/TLOonepager Mar2009.pdf>

Survivors Network of Those Abused By Priests. 'Miami Attorney Wins Unprecedented Sex Case Using 1868 Indian Treaty.' *SNAP Press Statement.* 29 Apr. 2009. Print.

Teehee, Kimberly. 'Forging a New and Better Future Together.' Office of Public Engagement. The White House. 21 Jul. 2010. Web. 12 Apr. 2011. <http://www.whitehouse.gov/blog/2010/06/21/forging-a-new-and-better-future>

Ternay, Andy. 'How to Rape a Woman and Get Away With It.' *Native American Net Roots.* 21 Jul. 2008. Web. 12 Apr. 2011. <www.nativeamerican netroots.net/diary/130/>

Timm, Jane C. 'VAWA Passes House, with Full Protections for LGBT, Native Americans.' *MSNBC,* 12 Sept. 2013. Web. 01 Oct. 2014 <http://www.msnbc.com/morning-joe/vawa-passes-house-full-protections>

Tjaden Patricia, and Nancy Thoennes. 'Full Report of the Prevalence, Incidence, and Consequences of Violence Against Women.' A study prepared at the National Institute of Justice, Office of Justice Programs. U.S. Department of Justice. NCJ 183781. Nov. 2004.

Toensing, Gale C. 'Indian-Killer Andrew Jackson Deserves Top Spot on List of Worst U.S. Presidents.' *Indian Country Today Media Network,* 20 Feb. 2012. Web. 01 Oct. 2014. <http%3A%2F%2Findiancountrytodaymedianetwork.com%2F2012%2F02%2F20%2Findian-killer-andrew-jackson-deserves-top-spot-list-worst-us-presidents-98997>

———. 'Obama Signs 'Historic' Tribal Law and Order Act., *Indian Country Today.* 30 Jul. 2010. Web. 12 Apr. 2011 <http://www.indiancountrytoday.com/home/content/Obama-signs-historic-Tribal-Law-and-Order-Act-99620099.html>

Trask, Haunani-Kay. 'Settlers of Color and 'Immigrant' Hegemony: 'Locals' in Hawai'i.' *Amerasia Journal.* UCLA Asian American Studies Center Press. (2000): 124.

Treaty with the Choctaw. 7 Stat., 333. 27 Sept. 1830. Print.

Treaty with the Wyandot, Delaware and Others. 7 Stat., 131. 8 Sept. 1815. Print.

'Tribal Law and Order.' *New York Times.* 1 Aug. 2010. Web. 12 Apr. 2011. < http://www.nytimes.com/2010/08/02/opinion/02mon3.html>

Tribal Law and Order Act. 18. U.S.C. § 115. 29 Jul. 2010. Print.

'Tribes Question 'Unfunded Mandate' From Tribal Law and Order Act.' *indianz.com.* 27 Aug. 2010. Web. 12 Apr. 2011. <http://64.38.12.138/News/2010/021398.asp>

United States Attorney's Office, District of Oregon. United States Department of Justice. 'Confederated Tribes Of The Umatilla Indian Reservation To Prosecute Domestic Violence Cases Under VAWA 2013 Pilot Project Allows Tribal Prosecution of Non-Indian Abusers For the First Time in More Than Three Decades'. 06 Feb. 2014. Web. 01 Oct. 2014. <http://www.justice.gov/usao/or/news/2014/20140206_vawa.html>

United States. Department of Justice. 'Indian Country Investigations and Prosecutions 2011–2012.' 2012. Print.

United States. Department of Justice. 'Indian Country Investigations and Prosecutions 2013.' 2014. Print.

'US Authorities Fail to Protect Native American and Alaska Native Women from Shocking Rates of Rape, Reports Amnesty International.' *Native American Times* 27 Apr. 2007: 1–2.

Venegas, Yolanda. 'The Erotics of Racialization: Gender and the Sexuality in the Making of California.' *Frontiers: A Journal of Women Studies*. 25.3 (2004): 63–89.

Vetter, William V. 'A New Corridor for the Maze: Tribal Criminal Jurisdiction and Nonmember Indians.' *American Indian Law Review*. 17.2 (1992): 349–456.

Vinzant, John Harlan. *The Supreme Court's Role in American Indian Policy*. El Paso: LFB Scholarly Pub., 2009. Print.

Violence Against Women Reauthorization Act of 2013. S. 47, 113 Cong. (2014) (enacted). Print.

'Violence Against Women Act (VAWA) Renewal Passes the House and Senate and Signed into Law.' Violence Against Women Act. *National Network to End Domestic Violence*, 2013. Web. 01 Oct. 2014. <http%3A%2F%2Fnnedv.org%2Fpolicy%2Fissues%2Fvawa.html>

Wang, Hansi Lo. 'For Abused Native American Women, New Law Provides A 'Ray Of Hope'' *NPR*. National Public Radio. 20 Feb. 2014. Web. 01 Oct. 2014. <http://www.npr.org/blogs/codeswitch/2014/02/20/280189261/for-abused-native-american-women-new-law-provides-a-ray-of-hope>

Washburn, Wilcomb E. *Red Man's Land/White Man's Law: The Past and Present Status of the American Indian*. 2nd Edition. Norman: University of Oklahoma Press, 1971.

Waters, Anne. 'Introduction: Indigenous Women in the Americas.' *Hypatia*. 18.2 (2003): ix–xx.

Weaver, Hilary. 'The Colonial Context of Violence.' *Journal of Interpersonal Violence*. 24.9 (2009): 1552–1563.

Wetzelbill. 'I Was Witness to One on My Reservation.' Comment on One in Three Native American Women Will Be Raped in Her Lifetime. 26 Jul. 2007. Web. 12 Apr. 2011 <democraticunderground.com>

White, Hallie Bongar, Kelly Gaines Stoner, and James G. White. '2008 Final Report: Creative Civil Remedies Against Non-Indian Offenders in Indian Country.' *Southwest Center for Law and Policy*. Tucson, Arizona. 2008.

Williams, Robert. *The American Indian in Western Legal Thought: The Discourses of Conquest*. New York: Oxford University Press: 1990.

Wilkinson, Charles F., and Christine L. Miklas. *Indian Tribes As Sovereign Governments: A Sourcebook on Federal-Tribal History, Law and Policy*. Oakland: AIRI, 1988.

Women Are Sacred Conference: Honoring Sacred Turtle Women. Sacred Circle. Oakland, CA. 12–14 Jun. 2009.

Yee, Jessica. 'How Native Women Built the Tribal Law and Order Act.' *Ms. Magazine Blog*. 3 Aug. 2010. Web. 01 Oct. 2010. <http://msmagazine.com/blog/blog/2010/08/03/the-woman-behind-the-tribal-law-and-order-act>

Zinn, Howard. *The People's History of the United States*. New York: HarperCollins, 2003.

CRITICAL INDIGENOUS AND AMERICAN INDIAN STUDIES

Andrew Jolivette
General Editor

The Critical Indigenous and American Indian Studies series welcomes highly innovative, inter-disciplinary manuscripts that explore the historic and contemporary experiences of American Indians, Alaska Natives, and Indigenous Peoples throughout Oceania and the Pacific. We seek submissions from scholars working on the following topics: literary studies, community/public health, languages and cultural preservation, cultural studies, gender and sexuality, politics and sovereignty, religion and philosophy, education, and media studies. This series seeks to increase the international presence of scholarly monographs written and published by American Indian and Indigenous Peoples that address indigenous people's rights as a matter of social justice and human rights.

For additional information about this series or for the submission of manuscripts, please contact:

Peter Lang Publishing
Acquisitions Department
29 Broadway, 18th floor
New York, NY 10006

To order other books in this series, please contact our Customer Service Department:

800-770-LANG (within the U.S.)
212-647-7706 (outside the U.S.)
212-647-7707 FAX

Or browse online by series at:

www.peterlang.com